Professional's Guide to Publicity

Third Edition

Richard Weiner

Other books by Richard Weiner:

Professional's Guide to Public Relations Services
News Bureaus In the U.S.
Syndicated Columnists
Military Publications
College Alumni Publications
Investment Newsletters

Library of Congress Catalog Card Number. 78-52626
ISBN 0-913046-07-8

Printed in the United States of America

Published by
Public Relations Publishing Co., Inc.
888 Seventh Avenue
New York, N.Y. 10106

CONTENTS

INTRODUCTION

This book is a work manual for the working publicist in dealing with the working press. Publicity is a difficult craft and its practice requires hard work. There are no guaranteed, precise, scientific programs which can be designed to achieve success, and even what constitutes "success" often is amorphous.

Many books, publications and courses about public relations include extensive discussions about publicity. This book does not include discussions on the art and theory of publicity, nor does it describe the media and other major aspects of public relations and communications.

Also omitted are detailed discussions of the art of news release writing and other types of publicity writing. This is covered in journalism textbooks, though publicists generally find that experience is the best teacher.

Extensive study and practice is necessary to develop a sense of correlation between what is useful both to the media and also the "source" of the publicity.

This book is the distillation of over 25 years of experience of a public relations practitioner who believes strongly that both novice and veteran publicists can develop more efficient skills. As a primer, it attempts to fill a void among the reference books in the field by providing a succinct compilation of "tips," rules, reminders and pragmatic advice. The manual therefore omits anecdotes, examples and dissertations in order for it to be most useful as a practical work guide.

Many of the rules and guidelines are subject to debate and the flexible, creative publicist develops personal rules and exceptions to the rules.

In the United States, a country in which advertising and public relations techniques are more common than anywhere else, many business executives and other sophisticated, intelligent people continue to confuse advertising and publicity. In other countries, the distinctions between advertising and publicity often are blurred and misunderstood to a greater degree than in the U.S.

Public relations practitioners sometimes also act as advertising agents and try to combine advertising and publicity. The two can work together, but it is important to understand the differences, as well as the similarities.

An advertisement, according to its dictionary definition, is "a public notice or announcement, usually paid for."

Publicity is defined as "any information or promotional material which brings a person, place, product or cause to the notice of the public."

It is obvious that, according to these definitions, publicity can include advertising and vice versa. In actual practice, the advertiser purchases space or time from the communications medium, whereas the publicist endeavors to obtain a news article or other space or time in media—without purchasing it.

Of course, the publicist is paid for his services, so the phrase "free publicity" as compared to "paid advertising" is misleading. However, technically, the publicity is "free," in that it is not purchased by the sponsor, as differentiated from advertising.

All this may seem basic and obvious to professional public relations practitioners. However, advertising and public relations are linked, and this often produces problems. One of the problems is that some advertisers think that their purchasing power with the media can help them to obtain "free publicity" as a fringe benefit, and, indeed, they can. It is regrettable to note that the separation between the news and advertising departments is violated at many publications throughout the world. It is a fact that many low-budget publications, such as trade and business journals, and many commercial broadcasting stations often favor advertisers. Large department stores and other big local advertisers do carry weight with the media.

This is a subject which is rarely discussed because it involves journalistic and public relations ethics. Frankly, there's nothing illegal or immoral in including a news release with an advertising insertion order, and some public relations practitioners do this.

However, it generally is not a desirable technique and certainly cannot be used when the publicity client is not an advertiser. In fact, the publicist sometimes succeeds in obtaining publicity only in the media in which the client advertises and ignores or fails to obtain publicity in other media.

Let's take another look at advertising and publicity to make sure we understand and appreciate their differences and similarities. Advertising is controlled by the client. The advertiser can obtain publication or broadcast of its message complete and verbatim. The advertisement will appear exactly as written by the client, on the exact date in the exact medium in which the advertiser desires, providing, of course, the advertiser pays for it and it meets mechanical and other specifications.

This controllability indeed is an asset. The advertisement can be preprinted or reprinted and used at point-of-sale and other promotion. Employees and customers can be told with confidence when and where the advertisement will appear. And, the advertisement can be repeated as often as desired.

On the other hand, publicity is not guaranteed or controllable. The most capable publicist rarely can predict with certainty when and where the publicity will appear. Nor can the publicity be repeated on a continuing basis in exactly the same form. However, when publicity does appear, it can have a greater impact than advertising, because the publicity represents a third-party endorsement by the media.

Indeed, it is more than just a coincidence to note that the media which have the greatest influence generally are those which have an editorial integrity. This integrity often is based on a separation between advertising and publicity.

The primary tool of publicity is the news release. A news release is not an advertisement. It is not even a thinly disguised advertisement. The news release is written and presented in a totally different manner from advertising. If the news release is to be utilized by the media and if it is to have a high degree of believability, the news release must be written in adherence to high journalistic standards.

Publicity can be an extremely frustrating business. A capable practitioner can do everything correctly and still not be able to see visible results. It is particularly exasperating to look at newspapers and other media and read what often seems to be trivia, puffery and articles which seem to have less reason for appearing in print than what the publicist sent to the media.

Always remember that the responsibility of the media is to its readers, listeners and viewers, and not to the publicist. Therefore, resist the impulse to suggest that the media cover your event or use your material by referring to something which already has appeared and is of lesser consequence, or something which already has appeared about a competing company or organization. Similarly, resist the impulse, which often takes place when something which you have sent to the media is not used, to send a snippy letter.

It is proper, and helpful, to meet with an editor, particularly a trade or business editor, in order to find out why something was not used and what the editor may be interested in. However, even the most helpful editor does not look at the problem from the viewpoint of the publicist and it simply does no good for the publicist to have an adversary relationship.

A constructive approach is to concentrate on improvement of professionalism, to the degree that is is possible. Sloppiness often creeps into the operations of major publicity departments and agencies. The conscientious publicist cannot attribute

3

frequent failures to the vagaries of the media. It often is possible to scrutinize day-to-day operations and find flaws and areas for improvement.

Since the publication in 1975 of the first edition of this book, several media changes have significant implications to publicists. The trend to vastly increased consumer-service articles and sections in major newspapers and magazines has opened up opportunities for product news releases, advice interviews and other publicity.

A new dimension in local TV news is ENG, electronic news gathering, which uses portable minicam equipment for live, on-the-air reports. More important to the publicist are the longer (one and two hours) local evening news programs, with consumer reporters and magazine-like formats which use features of the type formerly confined to daytime interview programs.

The wire services, major syndicates and many newspapers have converted to electronic transmission and typesetting, and news rooms now look like data processing centers, complete with VDTs (video display terminals). A few publicists are experimenting with news releases which are typed so that they can be fed directly into computers for editing on VDT screens. The typeface (e.g., Courier 12), format (no hyphenation, set margins, use of cross-hatch correction marks and other symbols, OCR film ribbon) and other modifications are relatively easy to accomplish. However, scannable news releases have not become popular and are not yet necessary.

In addition to revisions and insertions of new items in every chapter, several new sections have been added, including writing, telephone tips, a film glossary, and a description and evaluation of public relations periodicals.

The author hopes that this book will be useful, to beginning and experienced publicists, and hopes that readers will pass along additional tips, differences of opinion and comments for use in the next edition.

NEWS RELEASES

The primary means of communication between the publicist and the media is the news release (sometimes called a *handout*). When sending one or a relatively few copies of a news release, the simplest, most economical and most readable form is an original typed copy. Never—never—send a carbon copy. Of course, the use of Xerox or photocopies is acceptable.

Letters There is one situation in which a carbon is called for, and that is when sending a letter to a specific writer, reporter or departmental editor, and it is desirable to also inform another editor, particularly the city editor or other supervisor. A carbon copy of the letter is the logical way of making contact with more than one person at the publication or station and, at the same time, avoiding the accusation of trying to place the same story in two departments.

A situation which many publicists tend to forget about is the sending of a thank you letter to an editor after an article on which you have worked has appeared. In such cases, good press relations can be enhanced by sending a letter to the reporter involved or the carbon to his supervisor.

A little apple polishing, particularly when you call it to the boss's attention, never hurts. In fact, you occasionally can get extra mileage out of a thank you letter by sending it addressed to "The Editor," for publication in the "Letters to the Editors" column. This section generally appears on or near the editorial page of a newspaper and in the high-readership front pages of many business and consumer magazines.

In the case of a nonprofit organization, for example, the thank you letter can note how helpful the recently published article was to the organization. In other cases, it is relatively easy to find a point in the article which can be amplified, or to make a

5

newsworthy comment. This is much better than sending a correction or criticism, which is the most common form of follow-up letter to the editor.

Rebuttal letters generally should be avoided. Unless there has been a serious factual error or interpretation with which you strongly disagree, you're generally better off to simmer down and not risk a repetition of the charges or a printed rebuttal from the editor.

Editorials The letters-to-the editor column is one of several departments which is vastly underutilized by publicists. Another section of the newspaper, perhaps the most influential, is the editorial page, which offers at least two types of opportunities. One is the editorial written by the editor-in-chief or editor of the editorial page, and the other is that part of the editorial page, or the page adjacent to it, sometimes called the op-ed page, which contains by-lined articles, many of which are ghost-written or prepared by publicists.

One of the simplest techniques to suggest an editorial is to send a cover letter with a news release, indicating that the content of the news release may be the occasion for an editorial. It is not necessary to write the actual editorial, as the editorial writer prides himself in presenting his own ideas in his own way. However, it is not improper to include a suggested editorial. More likely, a fact sheet, particularly if there is a news release or other news peg alluded to in the cover letter, can be extremely helpful. Keep in mind that it is desirable to send the material to the editor several days prior to its distribution as a news release, even though the editorial quite likely will not appear until the same day or subsequent to the news release.

The editorial page is not sacrosanct, and publicists, particularly those for associations and nonprofit organizations, can avail themselves of the type of editorial which literally raises money or produces spectacular results.

In sending news releases to a specific editor, such as the women's or business editor, the alert publicist can obtain extra mileage by circling portions of the news release that may be of interest to other departments in the newspaper and sending it along with an appropriate cover note. This is a particularly good technique with regard to the chief editorial writer, who generally is looking for an item in the news which can serve as a springboard for comment. Similarly, though most columnists require advance exclusives, it sometimes is possible to obtain an entire column by a columnist based on a previously issued news release. The major consideration is simply to be familiar with the media. For example, it's sometimes possible to send a news release which has had extensive distribution to a radio or television commentator or program director, together with a cover letter which suggests the particular angle which will enable the broadcaster to make use of it.

Time Peg   The most desirable news peg is one which is inherent in the news release. However, the news tie-in can be related to a holiday, commemorative day, week or month, the season of the year or an anniversary. Check your almanac for dozens of ideas for timely occasions for news releases, features, editorials, scripts, tapes, films and other publicity techniques—all of which can be prepared in advance.

A "time-peg" is preferable, but not essential. In the interest of good media relations, and also to stimulate immediate results, a fact sheet, booklet, annual report, fact kit or other reference material can be distributed to editors, including editorial writers, with or without a news release.

For all publicity material, but especially for reference and other items which are likely to be retained, be sure to include the names of publicity contacts and their office and home telephone numbers, and package the items in a way in which they can be easily filed.

Press Kit   The most common folder used by publicists is the press kit folder which generally has its bottom edges folded up to produce pockets for the insertion of photos and other materials. A less used, but extremely economical and efficient technique, is an ordinary office file folder, manila or any other color, perhaps with an index sticker already affixed.

Another infrequently used technique which is amazingly simple and inexpensive is to prepare one or more 3 x 5 inch index cards, with a summary of the subjects, brand names or other highlights, plus, of course, office and home phone numbers of spokespeople. Some publicists produce these reference aids in assorted sizes, such as the smaller Rolodex card, in an attempt to anticipate the different file card systems of editors, but this probably is gilding the lily.

In the movie business, "press book" has a special meaning. A press book is a comprehensive collection of publicity, advertising and promotion materials about a single motion picture. It is provided by the producer to exhibitors (the owners and operators of theaters) for their local use. The press book generally includes background information (including the cast and other "credits"), articles, photos, suggested reviews, ads, displays and promotion suggestions. Also included are descriptions of posters and other materials which can be ordered. (The most common size of poster, called a two-sheet, generally is inserted in lobby showcases and used on easels.)

The press book generally is printed on glossy paper and looks like a tabloid newspaper. It is not a press kit, though the components of a press kit are included in the "book."

Release Format   Let's return now to our examination of the news release format.

One of the reasons for including an identification, which is called a slug line, at the top of each page, not only is to identify the pages should they become separated, but also because in some cases, each page is sent to different typesetters. Each page, which is called a "take," is part of the newspaper "copy." It is interesting to note that the different versions filmed of the same scene in motion pictures also are called takes.

The end of the last page is noted with a "30" or contains several asterisks or other symbols indicating the end of the story.

A good journalistic technique is to type the word "more" at the bottom of the page, set off by dashes before and after the word or positioned in the center of the line within parentheses. This indicates to the editor and typesetter that the news release continues on another page and is useful if pages get separated. Additional pages of a news release can be numbered at the top, or a journalistic phrase can be utilized in the upper left corner, such as "Add One" on the second page, "Add Two" on the third page, together with the slug line which simply is the key word of the story, its source, or other word or phrase which identifies the release.

One more addition to your journalism vocabulary is the word flimsy, which is a sheet of thin paper used by many newspaper reporters. A copy of the wire service, syndicate or newspaper article sometimes is provided to the public relations source, at the time it is written or afterward. When respectfully requesting this precious sheet of paper, it may help (a wee bit) to refer to it as a flimsy.

Headline   On the matter of headlines on news releases, some editors state that they do not like headlines, as this is a presumption on the part of the publicist in terms of indicating the news value of the story and how it should be headed, and even a reporter rarely writes his own headline. However, the purpose of the headline on a news release is not to compete with the publication's own headline writers, who indeed are specialized journalists, but rather to present a summary of the story in order to flag the attention of the editor as to the essence of the story. On balance, therefore, headlines can be extremely useful to the publicist and should not be omitted.

Instead of a headline on a news release, some publicists provide a one- or two-line summary in the upper left corner of the news release. Of course, one must avoid unintentional ambiguities in headlines, which occasionally slip into even the best-edited publications.

Corrections   When an error appears in a newspaper article, including an unintentional error in a caption or headline, an alert publicist sometimes can obtain a correction prior to the appearance of the last edition, but only when the publicist obtains the first or early edition and immediately calls the newspaper. Never call in a correction unless it is important and you are absolutely sure that your correction is accurate. In some cases, a harassed and busy editor will delete a story from subsequent editions, rather than rewrite it, so you have to decide whether the story being killed is preferable to the story continuing to appear in the same manner.

Occasionally—hopefully, it is only occasionally—a news release is sent out which contains an error. If the error is a minor one, such as misspelling or a typographical error, it rarely is necessary to issue a correction. The error should serve as a reminder, however, that news releases should be carefully proofread prior to typing and printing, and this is particularly important in releases with technical names or financial data. However, on those rare occasions when it is deemed necessary to issue a correction, the usual procedure is to telephone the correction, in order to make sure that the media do not use the incorrect information. In some cases, it is adequate to send out the correction by mail. In so doing, a good idea is to retype the entire corrected news release and indicate on the top something along the following lines: "The following news release is a corrected version of a news release sent to you yesterday."

The matter of correction is embarrassing, of course, but it is better to flag the mistake than to have it appear. Fortunately, factual errors are rare. The most common problems pertain to journalistic style.

Length   Most news releases tend to be too long. A news release rarely should run over two pages. In preparing a news release, a rough guideline is that about four to five lines of typing will produce, if reproduced verbatim, about an inch of newspaper type, assuming the conventional width, which is eight columns to a page.

Don't try to cram a long story on to one or two sheets of news release paper, or use unconventional lengths of news release paper, such as legal-sized sheets, rather than 8½" x 11" paper. Almost every publication is deluged with news releases and, while you may feel that your article is so newsworthy that it demands to be read, keep in mind that the temptation for the editor who is opening stacks of news releases on a daily basis is to scan and throw away the majority of them. An odd size may tend to catch his eye, but sometimes this can be on a negative basis.

Paper   Some publicists, particularly those in the fashion field, believe that special textures and colors of paper are consistent with their message, create an image and make their news releases more outstanding. This may be valid but rarely is worth the effort or expense. In fact, almost all editors, and particularly those who work with copy-desk pencils and office typewriters, really prefer the conventional sizes and types of news release paper, as it enables them to work directly on the paper.

As with all generalizations, particularly candid opinions and comments of this type, there are exceptions and variations. For example, a news release related to St. Patrick's Day might be printed on green paper.

Another point subject to debate is the matter of the use of a letterhead or specially printed news release paper. Some large organizations feel that such a paper is more likely to attract the attention of an editor and over a period of time, particularly if the content of the news release is good, will receive priority attention. This probably is an indulgence, and it is quite rare that such a news release would receive special attention. In fact, some specially printed release papers are so ostentatious that they call attention to the extravagance and commerciality of the publicist. More important, the letterhead portions of these papers take up excessive amounts of space. Therefore, the most straightforward procedure is merely to include the name, address and phone number of the publicist in the upper left corner of the first page.

Contact   News releases from public relations agencies should include the name, address and phone number of the agency, followed by a line,

For: (name of client)

In some cases, it may be desirable to include the address and phone number of the client.

It is amazing that many professional publicists do *not* include all of this information. In dealing with spot news, it often is desirable to include a night telephone line or home telephone number, particularly for those companies which have switchboards which close at 5 p.m. or other hour which is considered too early for many editors, particularly those on morning newspapers where the greatest activity is in the late afternoon and evening hours.

Another affectation is the use of specially printed news release envelopes. All mail to media is opened, and the larger the staff of the publication, the more likely is the mail to be opened by an assistant, on a mass basis, and the news release merely removed and stacked with others, regardless of the type of envelope in which it was mailed.

In going through stacks of news releases at major recipients of publicity, particularly newspapers, it is shocking to note the number from professional sources which are improperly typed, that is, those which are single-spaced or typed on both sides of the sheet. Always double-space news releases and, if possible, use wide margins or even triple-spacing. Never type or write on the reverse side of the paper. Amateurish releases are likely to be ignored. More important, those editors, particularly on trade publications, who work directly on the news releases, want to have room to do their editing on the release paper. This often means cutting, pasting, and rearranging paragraphs, which is awkward if anything appears on the reverse side.

The upper right corner should contain the release date, and this should be included even when the release is a feature article or other material which can be used anytime after receipt. A major reason for including the release date really is to inform the editor when the release was sent to other media, so that an editor who perhaps was away from his desk will know what is old and what is fresh. In other words, the usual procedure is simply to write "for immediate release," and then the date the release is being mailed out or the following day or the day after that.

Release Date   A preferred form with feature articles and others which do not have a specific time tag is to date the release *two* days after the day it is being mailed out. The reason for this is that even with the mails working at optimum conditions, the news release will be delivered the day after is is mailed and, with the exception of evening newspapers who receive it on that day, the earliest that a morning newspaper or any other publication could use the release is the following day, which is two days after the date it was mailed. Is all that clear?! If not, look at it this way. With the mails no longer operating at optimum efficiency, and with news releases increasingly being mailed over larger geographical areas, the dating of the release two days after it is mailed in a sense allows a larger number of publications to make use of it at the same time. Furthermore, the editor who receives it on the morning after it was mailed has that day in which to follow up and work on the news release. Thus, in some cases, it may be desirable to date the release even more than two days in advance, perhaps three or four, but not very much more than that because the tendency of the editor might be to use it prematurely or to discard it, though many editors do maintain "future files."

Though there are times when a Saturday, Sunday or holiday release date is desirable, the release date generally should be a weekday. Therefore, a release mailed on a Thursday or Friday generally should bear a release date for the following Monday.

Regardless of the way in which you decide when to mail a release and what date to use for the release date, be sure to include the release date. Of all the essential components of a news release, the most frequently omitted is the date.

The time of the day occasionally is included when the release refers to an event scheduled to take place at a specific time. Financial releases or others with "hard news" also may require the time of the day. However, the practice of "For A.M. release" or "For P.M. release," as a way of favoring morning or afternoon newspapers, is infrequently used. Not too many years ago, the general circulation morning newspapers in New York were the News, Mirror, Herald Tribune and Times, and they were intensely competitive with the afternoon dailies, the Post, Journal-American and World-Telegram. The situation was similar in Boston, Los Angeles and other major cities. Today, the competition has shifted from within the newspaper medium to newspaper vs. television.

Though the top of the news release generally states For Immediate Release, or For Release, or sometimes simply For Release At Will, it occasionally is necessary to distribute a release prior to a particular event or, for various other reasons, to date the release, Hold For Release Until— or For Release After—. Whenever possible, this form of predating should be avoided, as editors may utilize the material prior to the indicated time, sometimes inadvertently.

Mailing A very efficient approach, particularly for those organizations which mail out large numbers of news releases to a variety of media, is to mail out the *same* news release on different days. For example, the release can be mailed several days or a week in advance of the release date to weekly newspapers and other weekly publications. A few days later, mail the same news release to daily newspapers and reserve the last mailing, a day or two prior to the release date, for the radio and TV media, which work on the most current basis. In that way, each of the media is treated equally in terms of recognizing their particular deadlines. When possible, mail to columnists, particularly those who write for syndicates and wire services, as well as the weekly news magazines and Sunday supplements, should be sent several weeks prior to the news release date. Some sections of major Sunday newspapers close as much as six days prior to publication, and, again, an early mailing can be extremely helpful. And, of course, magazines close many weeks or months prior to publication.

Features, backgrounders and other publicity material in which the specific release date is not vital sometimes are dated at the end of the release, to indicate the date of mailing. In such cases, an alternate form is to indicate only the month (and year).

Because of the vagaries of mail delivery, it sometimes is desirable to mail a news release and *also* to service it by messenger or one of the Teletype services. Telegrams are rarely used because of delivery problems, possibility of garbling of the text and the cost.

One of the most efficient, and least used, means of news release transmission is to deliver it yourself. When the occasion warrants, try it. Sedentary executives can benefit from the exercise and the learning experience. Many top-level practitioners have forgotten what a newspaper city room looks like, and it's generally an exciting, and rewarding, experience to hand-deliver a news release. True, security guards and receptionists are barriers to entrance at some newspapers, wire services, radio and television stations, but it's worth a try, even if you end up by merely telephoning from the reception room.

The largest Teletype service in the publicity field is PR Newswire, which can transmit a news release directly to several hundred major publications and stations, with incredible accuracy and at a cost far below that of telegraph or messenger service. Ironically, PR Newswire recently was acquired by Western Union.

In sending out press advisories or other invitations to attend events, the question arises as to when is the best time to send out the invitation, as publicists often are concerned about sending out the invitation either too early or too late. As with many other news releases which are handled on a mass basis, it frequently is necessary to break up the list into two or more categories, so that magazines and other nondaily media are likely to receive the invitation earlier than the broadcast media, daily newspapers and others which generally are not interested in events which are more than a day or two ahead of their current assignment log. Publicists who spend hundreds of hours organizing an event sometimes do not want to put in the extra time to break up their lists in this manner.

Another solution to this thorny problem is to send out an invitation considerably in advance of the event, that is, about two weeks prior to the event, and then send out the same or a follow-up invitation with more detailed information a couple of days prior to the event. With regard to the last-minute invitation, don't forget to allow an extra day or two for the occasional postal delays, as well as the fact that the recipient may not be in the office every day.

Telephone   Publicists often are reluctant to follow up mailed invitations with telephone calls, for fear of harassing the editor. It indeed is embarrassing to call for the purpose of asking the editor if he received your letter or news release or invitation, but it often is necessary and, surprisingly, the response sometimes is "No, tell me about it!"

In summary, personal two-way communication, such as via the telephone, generally is the quickest, most economical and most effective. Don't be shy. It's part of your job. Don't be afraid to pick up the telephone. Not everything can be handled on a mass, impersonal basis.

Dateline   News releases which have a specific time relevance sometimes are handled by putting the day on which the news release is distributed on the first line of the news release, which is called the dateline. However, this procedure is relatively rare for the bulk of publicity material, particularly feature articles or news releases distributed locally.

The dateline properly consists of the city of origin and the date the article is transmitted. The state or country is included if the city alone otherwise would be unclear. Following are a few examples.

WASHINGTON, Sept. 10—
BALTIMORE, May 10—
NEW YORK, Jan. 1—
PEKING, Feb. 6—
AMMAN, Jordan, Aug. 12—
MIDDLETOWN, Conn., June 4—

Note that only the city is set in all-capital letters. It is not necessary to include D.C. in stories emanating from our nation's capital or to include the state in New York City datelines. The month is abbreviated where possible, and the year is omitted.

The dateline sometimes looks like an affectation by a publicist who is overly striving to make a news release look professional. It usually is redundant, is not the style of newspapers with regard to local stories and becomes somewhat complicated when sending out news releases prior to events. Thus, in an attempt to

13

add a professional touch, the publicist sometimes can confuse the editor by making the news release look as if it is several days old by the time it is received.

Another reason for *not* putting the date on the first line is the fact that the first lines of the news release are the most precious to the publicist, as this is the part which likely will determine whether the editor will read further or throw away the news release. Why waste half the first line when you can start with the news!

Within a news release, whenever a reference is made to a day (e.g., today, tomorrow) insert in parenthesis the day of the week, so that is is clear. It's often a helpful reminder to insert the date in addition to the day of the week, in order to avoid confusion.

The Five W's There is a trend to the use of feature style news releases, including quotations, poetry and humor in the lead sentence, paragraph or paragraphs. Yet, the most common procedure still is the inverted pyramid, in which the key information is included at the top and subsequent paragraphs serve to expand the story. It is not essential to answer all five of the W's, who, what, where, when and why, in the first paragraph, but this bromide still applies to many news releases. It is confounding to note that news releases which should include vital information often inadvertently do not, and it's not coincidental that the best writers of feature news releases often are those who have been trained first in the writing of "straight" news releases. In other words, once you have learned how to write in the traditional fashion, you are much more likely to violate some or all the rules, and do it with ease and success.

One final word about that precious first line of the news release. An old newspaper axiom is not to start a sentence with a number. One reason for this is that a numeral at the beginning of a lead sentence could be confused with the dateline. However, the number could be spelled out in such cases. Furthermore, publicists should not fret about problems which can be solved easily by copy editors and typesetters. The way a news release is typed can be important, and there are many reasons for typing a news release more than once. A typist with publicity experience can be extremely helpful in producing news releases which conform to good journalistic style and not just in avoiding spelling and grammatical errors. For example, a typist can be on the lookout for "widows."

A widow is a line in a news release or publication which has only a few words so that the bulk of the line appears blank. Makeup editors try to avoid excessive use of widows and, to the extent that it is possible, publicists also should try to avoid them, particularly at the bottom of a page, as news releases often can be typed on one page, rather than one and one-quarter pages, without producing a crammed appearance. This may mean retyping or typing by a typist who is experienced with news releases, but over a period of time these savings, particularly in the case of news releases which are produced in quantities of hundreds, can make the effort worthwhile.

Style Dictionaries, stylebooks (The New York Times, The Associated Press and Ayer all are excellent) and other reference aids are essential for both the publicity writer and the typist. Secretaries in publicity operations often function as grammarians and editors and rarely are fully appreciated for their daily contributions.

The best secretaries are guided, but not bound, by rules. For example, the U.S. Postal Service has a recommended list of abbreviations, which are used for efficient addressing of envelopes, but should not be used for news releases. The average reader will recongize NY, NJ and a few others but is not likely to identify AK, CT, HI, MI and MT as Alaska, Connecticut, Hawaii, Michigan and Montana. When in doubt, spell out.

Another confusing area is the use of quotation marks or underlining to identify publications or other titles or special phrases. They often are unnecessary and can be confusing when there is an apostrophe within the quote. For example, instead of:
"Farm Editors' Forum,"
drop the quotes, if it's necessary to use the apostrophe after the second word.

A news release which can be sent intact to the typesetter certainly is desirable, but the primary objective is to concentrate on the content and style most likely to be useful to the editor or broadcaster, not the printer.

For this reason, it sometimes is helpful to break up a long news release by inserting subheads or titles in various places within the news release. The editor will eliminate these subheads, but they serve to make the release more readable and to point up key phrases.

One place where a blank space is desirable is at the top of the first page. Perhaps the second most common error (after omission of release dates) is to start the text of the release too close to the top of the page.

The body of a news release should start at least three spaces below the headline so that the editor may use this blank space for instructions to the copy editor or typesetter.

Paper clips present a variety of bedeviling problems with regard to publicity uses. For example, news releases and other publicity materials which run more than one page should be stapled in the upper left corner, rather than held together by use of paper clips, as it is simply too easy for papers to come apart and separate. Especially avoid the use of paper clips in connection with photos, unless the paper clip is carefully placed in a margin, as impressions of paper clips are likely to cause imperfections in the photo. Trade publication and newspaper editors are not likely to take the time to airbrush or eliminate these imperfections.

Staples, datelines, headlines and release dates are merely

details. The most siginficant aspect of a news release is its content. Beautifully produced news releases may score top grades in techniques, but the primary consideration is the content. The two key questions are:

1. Is the news release (or other publicity communication) newsworthy and of interest to the recipient?
2. Is it well-written and complete? In the final analysis, the publicist must ask the most critical question: Should this release be sent at all?

PHOTOS

Of the many skills required for success in publicity, writing ability invariably is the most important. Regretfully, not all publicists are good writers.

Even the poor writers generally are aware of the importance of rewriting and editing and often try to improve the quality of their news releases. However, when it comes to photos, most publicists, including the good writers, tend to become sloppy and even amateurish. As a result, tons of publicity photos are discarded by editors, representing a tremendous waste of money and loss of prized publicity opportunities. As with a news release, a good publicity photo consists of the sum of a multitude of details.

For example, it is assumed that a publicity photo will be cropped, that is, reduced and edited in various ways, by the photo editor. However, a reflection of the limited knowledge of photography by publicists is the fact that most publicists order full-sized prints from contact proof sheets without bothering to do any cropping. The creative publicist, working with a creative professional photographer, can do cropping at this early stage, in terms of eliminating extraneous matter and background material. This enhances the likelihood of the picture being used, by making it appear as tight and dynamic as possible, and also shows the editor what the picture is likely to look like.

Some publicity photos do not have borders, and this sometimes can be dramatic. However, a border can enhance the appearance, enable easy handling and provide a space for a small caption to be affixed. In this regard, and in dozens of other ways, publicists have neglected attempts to improve the creativity and efficiency of photos, and the result is that more money often is wasted on publicity photos than news releases.

Caption   Publicity photo mailings consist of more than just the photo,

17

and perhaps the most neglected detail is the caption.

The purpose of the caption is to identify the picture, and information included on the caption should be brief, factual and, of course, completely accurate.

There is a kind of cat and mouse game often played by publicists and media people with regard to the "plug" or credit. The art of the skillful publicist often comes into play most dramatically in the setting up of a photo. The trick is to include the product or other credit in such a way as to be an inherent part of the photo—too important to be cropped out and yet not so obvious as to be blatantly commercial or offensive. The same skill should be put to work in the writing of the caption.

A few publicists attach two captions to a photo. One, which sometimes is quite brief and merely generally identifies the photo or gives the names of the people in the photo and, most important, the name, address and phone number of the publicist, is pasted on the back of the photo, thus becoming a permanent part of the identification. This procedure is infrequently used, as it means an added cost, and some editors do not want anything on the back of the photo. It is possible, of course, to carefully affix a thin strip of identification or even use a rubber stamp, as some photographers do.

The second type of caption, which is more common and important, is affixed to the front of the photo. As with a news release, the name, address and phone number of the source should appear in the upper left corner. It is astounding that many publicists provide this information routinely on all news releases, but omit it from the caption, particularly in those cases where a photo accompanies a news release. Always remember that items can become separated and, in the case of major media, the news release and photo may be handled by different people and even different departments. And don't forget to include the date on the caption!

The general procedure in affixing the caption sheet, which usually is typed horizontally in the case of horizontal photos and in the conventional vertical manner in the case of vertical photos, is to utilize a short sheet, generally half-sized, as compared to the 8½ x 11 news release paper. However, it is possible to use a full-size sheet, and many publicists believe that this is desirable, as it serves as a protective cover for the entire photo.

Never affix a caption to the photo with a staple or paper clip, as the caption probably will be torn off by the editor. The most common procedure is to paste the lower part of the caption on the back of the photo, then fold the caption up over the photo, so that the typed portion of the caption is facing the photo, and the blank part of the caption sheet is facing the outside. The reason for this procedure is to enable the editor to unfold the caption, and, in so doing, the typed portion of the caption will appear immediately below the photo, as it does when published. The editor can identify the photo and, if desired, rewrite the caption directly on the caption sheet, as sometimes is done with a news release.

A few publicists have suggested that a preferable procedure is to type the caption so that it appears face up, and the blank side is affixed adjacent to the photo. Their reasoning is that this enables the editor to immediately see the caption information without unfolding the photo. This may be creative reasoning, but is is not valid because it is more important that the editor see the photo rather than the caption. Of course, this idea could be carried to its extreme by typing the caption information on both sides of the sheet. However, there are limits one can go to accommodate the editor, and the important point is that the caption identifies the photo, and the primary focus should be on the photo.

Cost   The sending of photos is considerably more expensive than news releases. First, there's the cost of the photography, then the cost of making prints, printing and affixing captions and, finally, the considerable cost of mailing, particularly since a captioned photo, generally accompanied by a news release, requires one or more sheets of cardboard backing. Because of the increased cost of postage, some mailers now use plastic sheets which are especially prepared for use by publicists. Plastic weighs a bit less than cardboard and may provide more effective protection. Finally, the envelopes cost considerably more than letter-size envelopes. A few mailers use cardboard envelopes, instead of cardboard inserts.

All of this might seem like dealing in pennies, but if the total cost is about 25 cents more than with a news release, as easily can be the case because of current postage costs, and the mailing totals only a hundred, this means an added cost of $25. Quite often, when one includes the cost of photography, the cost is considerably more.

Most publicists do not bother to break up their mailings into categories which receive only a news release and those which receive a news release with a photo. This is easily done, and certainly should be done in the case of publicatons such as The Wall Street Journal, which never use photos, as well as the many newsletters and other publications which also do not use photos. Even if the publication does use photos, the publicist should use his judgment with regard to whether there's a remote chance that a photo will be used. It's not just a matter of saving money, but also operating efficiently so that editors are not sent extraneous material in which they have little or no interest. Do this continuously and it can "turn off" an editor and diminish the chances of other, more relevant, material being used.

Some publicists note on a news release that a photo is available, and sometimes a list of available color and black and white photos is provided. This is a particularly good procedure in mailings involving fashion and feature subjects, in which

19

those editors who are interested in photos are likely to request them.

ID's   The captions accompanying photographs usually do not have headlines, though they can, providing the caption remains brief. A one-line identification at the top of a caption, sometimes referred to as the cut line, can suffice as a headline.

If it is necessary to include a great deal of information with the photo, it is preferable to include a news release together with the captioned photo. In fact, this is a good procedure anyhow. In many cases, publicists at news events distribute captioned photos to photographers and omit the news release. Photographers often work independently of the accompanying reporters and are "on the run," and should be given a fact sheet or news release.

Publicity photos, particularly those which are mass-reproduced, generally do not credit the photographer. The naming of a photographer is a courteous procedure and can be handled in the form of a parenthetical addition at the end of the caption.

Even more so than with news releases, brevity is the key word in captions. It is not necessary to try to be cute or even to write in complete sentences, but rather to provide the proper identifications, paying careful attention to the correct spelling of the names of the individuals in the photos and to their proper locations, that is, left to right. Where there are several individuals or more than one row, you may identify them by indicating such phrases, in parentheses, as, wearing a hat, sitting, standing or holding a plaque, in other words, anything to make sure that the recipient of the photo knows who's who. The key function of the caption is for identification purposes. Don't try to rewrite the accompanying news release. The exception, of course, is the captioned photo in which the caption is the entire news release.

One of the primary responsibilities of a publicist at news photo occasions is to make sure of the proper spellings of the individuals and the order in which they appear, from left to right, as seen from the camera's, or viewer's, eye. This is particularly important if there is a last-minute substitution of people, as compared to the advance notice sent to the media, or if the people appear in a different order. Don't assume that someone will be able to identify the people after the pictures are developed, and don't be afraid to walk up to prominent people and ask for their names.

A clever technique is to jot down some kind of notation, such as, beard, mustache, wearing tweed jacket, glasses or heavy necklace, so that you can be absolutely sure when you prepare the captions, particularly in the case of pictures which are processed and serviced the same day.

Remember also to obtain the addresses of all individuals shown in photos, particularly in the case of events where you do not know the individuals.

Procedures vary with regard to the signing of release forms, and this usually is not necessary in the case of news events.

In writing out the caption information for photographers and television cameramen, try to print or write legibly, using index cards or other surfaces on which you can write easily, particularly since in most cases you have to work under adverse, rushed conditions. One trick is to type up all of the names and identifications on a sheet of paper or card and then put a number next to each name, in accordance with the order in which they are standing, seated or shown in the photo, with number one indicating the individual furthest to the left.

Composition   The setting up of the subject matter of a photo is tremendously important. A great deal of training and attention is given to the writing and rewriting of news releases, but far less attention is given to the setting up of photographs and scenes which are likely to be useful to the photo and television media. Most photos distributed by publicists are dull, inanimate and much more likely to be tossed away than news releases, even though the cost of photos, simply in terms of their mechanical reproduction, is far greater.

For example, the number of photographs which are distributed by publicists containing large groups of people, rather than the generally accepted maximum of three or four, is legion.

Perhaps the most common type of publicity photo subject is the presentation of a plaque, trophy, certificate, check or other item, resulting in the most hackneyed type of photo, that is, several individuals looking down at the item being passed from one person to another. There are several ways to improve this type of photo.

First, don't have the individuals look *down*. Advise the participants to "cheat" by looking at the camera or slightly to the side, but, in no case should they look down so that their eyes appear shut. More important, figure out some kind of prop, such as an enlarged blowup of the check, or other item to make the photo a bit different and also to make the numerals on the check or the text of the plaque more readable.

Photos can be enlivened in many ways to enhance the chance of publication. Have you thought about, for example, hand-lettering the amount of money on a T-shirt or some other humorous fashion, or asking one of the individuals to hold up his fingers indicating the round number of thousands or millions, or attaching the check to a balloon, pair of scissors or other prop. No matter how staid the occasion, don't ignore the possibility of using a child or pretty girl or someone, be it "cheesecake" or not, to add a bit of glamour or human interest to the photo.

More important, the faces do not have to be somber, particularly if it is a joyous occasion, such as a presentation of a check, and there is an opportunity for some kind of display of spontaneous emotion, especially if it's that of glee. Take a look at

21

the newspapers and magazines which you respect and note the photos which they utilize. Sure, there are lots of head shots and other dull pictures, but, quite likely, more of those kinds of pictures were discarded than the pictures which convey some action or emotion and evoke the mood of the occasion.

An offbeat way to photograph a meeting in which there is a monotonous succession of speakers at a lectern is to position the photographer to the rear or side of the speaker, so that the other people at the dais or on the platform or a part of the audience, are shown in the background. Sometimes, there is more animation in the audience, such as a stockholder asking a question from the floor, and this type of photo has greater human interest than the conventional shot of a stand-up speaker. Perhaps the dreariest, least usable photos are people at banquet tables, but even these situations can be enlivened by the photographer on the lookout for the kinds of pictures which the wire services and major newspapers regularly use.

Pre-Photography

Advance planning of photos is often ignored by experienced publicists. For example, an alert publicist should arrange to have a banner, sign or other means of identifying the organization prominently displayed in the background or perhaps on the lectern, in the case of photo sequences that are taken at banquets and other occasions for speeches. Hotel and airline publicists are adept at working in the names of their organizations, and it often is possible to work in the name of the sponsor of the occasion—but it can only be done with advance planning.

The alert publicist should come prepared with adhesive tape and other materials, so that even with advance planning he can improvise in accordance with the particular circumstances, especially with regard to outdoor presentations and other impromptu scenes that are set up for photographers.

The old rule of a pretty girl, a dog or a child enhancing a photo still is a good one, and there are countless other ways to liven up an otherwise routine presentation. For example, even at the risk of insulting the participants, where one is stuck with a group of very old or unattractive people, surely it might be possible to figure out a way to involve the audience, such as the recipients of the charity, or in some way to liven up the photo and increase the chance of it being used.

Another possibility is not just to think in terms of a single photo, but rather some kind of two- or three-picture sequence. In dealing with a large number of VIP participants, you thus tactfully can break up the group of people into some kind of before, during or after sequence, or other photo sequences which tell a story.

Type up the number of words which fit into a column inch, then count up the number of column inches occupied by, for example, a five-column by six-inch photo, with its caption. This is the origin of the old saying that one picture is *literally* worth a thousand words. Now and then, isn't it worth an extra effort to get a thousand words of publicity? Incidentally, a full column holds about a thousand words of type.

Go back now to the setting up of the group photo. Don't abdicate your responsibility to the participants or the photographer. You are the director and should work in concert with the photographer.

The alert publicist who knows as much as he should about photography should carefully scrutinize the individuals being photographed, even if they are VIP's, and it would seem imprudent to rearrange them. For example, keep in mind that sunglasses are likely to photograph as dark spots, and one can request that they be removed. Similarly, hats generally should not be worn by men or women, as they are likely to cast shadows. Of course, if the client makes sunglasses or hats, or if these items are relevant, this advice is not applicable.

In a groundbreaking photo in which the individuals are wearing construction hats, tilt the hats back on their heads, so that their shadows and brims do not obscure the faces, and ask the individuals to look up so that their faces can be seen.

Many photographs require expensive retouching, and a newspaper may not want to spend the money to eliminate shadows. However, where you are taking your own pictures, you have an opportunity—even after the photo is taken—to transform unsuitable pictures into those which are likely to be used. For example, simply ask the photo developer or retoucher to put a piece of cardboard over the face of a person in a group picture who shows up too dark. This process, which is called dodging, can lighten the face so that it shows up at about the same level of density as others in the picture. A good photographer automatically does these kinds of tricks, but is is amazing how few publicists are aware of the fact that newspapers require pictures which are strong in black and white contrast, with an uncluttered background.

One of the problems in photographing ceremonial events, particularly luncheons, is that the client or other VIPs often will insist that others be rounded up to be included in the photo. As a result, the publicist is stuck with a picture with far too many people in it. One solution is to take extra pictures and provide these complimentary prints to the people in the photos, but not send them to the media. Another solution is to break up a large group into several small groups, and then send the photo to the hometown newspaper of the individuals in the photo or, in various other ways, divide up the media lists.

Another advantage of different poses is that it enables the publicist to offer each publication photos which are exclusive or relatively exclusive. The taking of a variety of photos also enables the publicist to provide editors or other media representatives attending the event with raw, undeveloped film directly from the event. The cost of film is one of the smallest expense items, and it is worthwhile to give an entire roll to any editor who requests it or even to photographers who are covering the event for the media, so that they can have additional photos.

Size   The conventional size photoprint used in publicity is 8 x 10 inches. However, it is possible to use a smaller size, such as 5 x 7. A procedure which is rarely used by publicists, however, is to use sizes larger than 8 x 10, and, in some cases, this is desirable. An 11 x 14 matte-finish photo of an individual, particularly when sent to a magazine, may be used, because it demonstrates to the editor several things, one of which is that the picture is sufficiently good that it can be overly enlarged in this manner without distortion and thus is likely to be even better when reproduced in smaller size in the publication.

Photoprints used by publicists generally are glossy prints. However, in some cases, it is preferable to use a less glossy surface, such as a matte or semi-matte dull finish, which, though not useful for newspapers, is much more likely to be utilized by magazines which have superior photo reproduction processes. Particularly in the case of food, fashion and show business photos, large sizes and superior reproduction may be spectacularly successful. Double-weight paper costs a bit more, but is better looking and avoids curling.

8 x 10 glossy photos should have a white margin around them to allow the editor to indicate his cropping marks. In sending special-size photos, such as 4 x 5 and 5 x 7, the margin may be omitted. It sometimes is desirable to enclose a small-size print in a cellophane envelope to enable it to be filed without being lost. Some publicists enclose all of their prints in envelopes to protect the prints from being scratched, but this is a service which is not essential.

In sending out product photos or other photos in which it may not be obvious which side is up, indicate this by means of an arrow or other device. It is these little extra thoughts which not only create good relations with the media, but enhance the likelihood of your material being used.

One economical advantage of a 4 x 5 photograph, which is permissible, particularly in the case of personnel photos, not only is the saving in the photo cost, but also a considerable saving in the mailing cost, as this size photo can be mailed in a #10 business envelope. Don't press your luck, though, by omitting the cardboard backing, even if it's only a small strip the size of the photo. Another variation is to paste a small-size photo on an 8 x 10 cardboard, preferably white, thus enabling use of a regular-size caption.

Lab Work   In addition to the use of copy-editing proofreading symbols, the publicist should become familiar with the code marks which are used to indicate cropping and other editing of photos. For example, close hash lines indicate "make darker," while small dots or circles indicate "make lighter." A straight line is used to indicate the outer limits of specific cropping, and wiggly lines generally indicate routine cropping, together with such notations as "crop for subject matter," "use your judgment," "full negative," "full paper size." All of these notations can be made with red crayon on a photoprint or contact proof. Negatives should never be marked and should be handled with utmost care.

Color   Quite a few newspapers now use run-of-paper (ROP) color, and some publicists, particularly those who work with food and fashion, distribute type-C color prints and color transparencies. This is expensive and is rarely utilized for mass mailings. A more common procedure is to query the women's or other editor as to whether color is desired, particularly since magazines and major newspapers are much more likely to use their own photographers for color prints.

An advantage of the type-C print over color transparencies is the ease with which these color prints may be retouched, though newspapers rarely retouch publicity photos, except to remove displays of blatant commercialism.

Wire services, syndicates and magazines generally prefer to receive a color negative, rather than a print, to insure exclusivity and also to facilitate production. A black-and-white negative may be requested, for the same reasons. Magazines generally prefer a transparency or color positive. A color negative and print can be provided to newspapers.

In many cases, particularly at news events, it is cheaper, faster and more efficient to provide the publication with a roll of film, developed or undeveloped.

Photo Sheet   Another rare technique, which should be used by more publicists, is to distribute a photo page, in mat or offset form, which is useful for weekly and small daily newspapers. Editors who require glossy photos may order them, in black and white or color, from these clip sheets, as they are called.

Black and white photo sheets sharply printed on glossy proof paper are suitable for reproduction by newspapers which print by the photo-offset process. Many suburban dailies and weeklies thus are able to use the proof sheet.

Color proof sheets often are printed on newsprint paper to show the editor how the photos reproduce, as well as to provide suggested layouts. An accompanying business reply postcard or order form enables the editor to order the exact type of printing material, including:

> direct casting mat, with prepositioned illustration and text
> reproduction proof
> scotchprint proof
> screened negatives
> transparency

The process can get quite complicated. For example, an editor can provide a sample of the newspaper's regular page-size layout, so that mats or other items can conform to column width and other specifications. The most convenient procedure is to provide transparencies from which the publication can make its own separations and plates.

Because of the extraordinary costs and complexities of color photos, a specialized service often is employed. Color requires a great deal of extra time and money, but can be worth the effort.

Similarly, the use of a good professional photographer and laboratory is essential. This does not necessarily require more money.

The conventional ferro-type glossy print still is the most common, as are machine-produced prints. Depth of contrast is reduced, and print tone is flattened out, so the need for good-quality photography is mandatory. The end product of the laboratory cannot be better then the input, the negative, though a custom laboratory can remove scratches, dust, lint, spots, specks and minor flaws in the negative by "spotting" each print with a tiny brush. These services sometimes are performed at no extra charge and is one more reason for a publicist to develop a knowledge of photography.

The more you explain the job to the photographer and the lab, the more they are likely to produce superior pictures. Try to specify how you plan to use the pictures, that is, the type of media, and how you envision the pictures should look.

When you get the contact sheet, ask the photographer for recommendations about the specific frames and manner of cropping and development. A lab occasionally can "push" a picture, that is, develop it under special conditions to increase its sensitivity rating. Therefore, don't hesitate to ask the photographer for information about the film and ASA rating. (The most common is Kodak Tri-X at its standard rating of ASA 400.)

It is assumed that you will not use prints which have developer, or "hypo," stains or other flaws, such as bubbles, spots, specks, wrinkles and creases, and that you will not have to cope with film which is overexposed, underexposed, improperly focused or poorly photographed or developed.

That's why you must work with top-quality professionals and why you must know more about photography than do most publicists.

The contact sheet is exposed for average quality of its many frames, whereas the individual print, made from an individual negative, is likely to be distinctly superior. The final print should be sharp, snappy, alive, crisp, clean, with a full range of tonal details, and not dull, flat, dusty, muddy, grainy, soft, gray, raw, dead. On a clear day, a clear picture is a joy to behold for the publicist and the photo editor.

In summary, publicists who pay considerable attention to news releases treat captions and photos cavalierly, and that is one reason that a larger percentage of publicity photos go unused, as compared to news releases. The principal reason, however, is the fact that most publicity photos are poorly planned and are dull. Even the traditional portrait photo, sent out with personnel appointment news releases, can be considerably more creative than the bulk of the photos now being sent. It is not necessary to use an extremely high-priced celebrity portrait photographer, though certainly one should not compromise in an attempt to save money by using an amateur or semiprofessional photographer.

It seems rather obvious to note that Polaroid pictures and snapshots should not be used by publicists, though some editors report receiving such photos, which are difficult or impossible to reproduce. The trend among many publications is to use smiling faces and informal poses, as compared to the more traditional, somewhat grim, expressions which flood the desks of society and business editors.

Machine Prints In the mass distribution of photos, you may want to save money by making a "copy negative" and prints from the copy negative, at a cost of about 19 cents a print, as compared to $1 or more which a photographer would charge for original prints. This is quite acceptable, though keep in mind that in making prints, these copy negatives can lose about 25% of their original definition, so that it is particularly important that the original prints be sharp and with strong contrasts between blacks and grays.

To repeat the obvious, photos must be handled carefully, with cardboard backing, and with attempts not to smudge, crack or bruise them. Experienced publicists, who really do know better, often use paper clips or write on the cover sheets, thus marring or damaging the photos. If you must write on the back of the photo, use the border or a peripheral area.

In handling photos, try to avoid getting fingerprints on them, and if you must write on the back of the photo, it generally is preferable to use a grease pencil or to write on a tissue or paper and then affix this to the photo.

In making mass mailings of anything, but especially photos, put your own name on the mailing list. This is an excellent way to check up on your in-house or outside mailing service and to determine the time of delivery and extent of damage, if any. More important, scrutinize the material, including proofreading, to make sure it was produced as you had intended. Photoprints, even those made by economical copy-print processes, should not be spotted, streaked or faded.

Mailing The sign of a mature executive is one who delegates responsibility. Many publicists therefore assign the responsibility for mailings to assistants, secretaries, clerks and mailing services. This is fine—when everything works well. When there are snafus, the publicist should make whatever changes are necessary, such as setting up checklists and proofreading procedures. Errors are made in all fields. What is most distressing is that some publicists are not aware of the errors and faulty procedures in their own operations, and this probably applies more to photos than news releases.

The photography at special events often is of very poor caliber. It is exasperating to note that many hundreds or thousands of dollars are spent on the setting up of special events, and, though one of the primary goals of these events is publicity, the matter of photography is grossly overlooked. Of course, a primary rule is to use a professional photographer and to make extensive arrangements with regard to the developing and servicing of the photos whenever and wherever you want them. For example, Associated Press, United Press and other organizations maintain commercial departments which are capable of turning out captioned prints within hours after the photos are taken. In spite of this, photos often are hastily taken in an unplanned manner, and then, regardless of how quickly they are developed, the end result is unusable.

Posing   One reason for this is that the partcipants in the photo often are top-level executives who either feign modesty or are involved in the details of the event and give little respect to the amount of time that the publicist and photographer must have access to them. There is little that can be done about this except to plan as much as possible in advance and also to include in the planning the setting up of as many pictures as possible prior to, during or even after the event.

There are few photos worse than those of a group of people sitting at a long table, such as a dais. Instead, gather the people that you want in your photos to the side of the room immediately *before* they sit down. Don't wait until after the event because the principals often make hasty exits.

Set up the pictures in a way in which they will be well-composed. In so doing, keep in mind what you'd like to have in the caption and, for example, try to have the principal person on the left, so that his is the first name which appears in the caption.

In other situations, group together people from the same organization so that in writing the caption the titles and affiliations can be simplified.

A factor which is often ignored is which side of the subject should face the camera. Most people have a good profile and a poor one, and the publicist, in conjunction with the photographer, should endeavor to pick the more flattering side. Many photographs show executives who not only do not look their best, but who have not had the benefit of someone straightening a tie, smoothing a jacket or in various other ways, doing what would have been done had the picture been taken in a studio. True, it often is not possible to take pictures at these events with as good lighting and composition as in a studio, but the publicist and photographer should try to think of the picture in terms of its composition.

For example, the center of interest can be in the left foreground of the picture, rather than in the center. This not only allows for cropping, but allows for a most artistic composition.

A procedure sometimes utilized by the publicity departments of large organizations is to provide a file number on the back of a photo and/or the caption, as well as at the end of a news release. This facilitates the ordering of additional photos and is important in the case of trade and business publications which may want a photo for use in a roundup article months or years after the photo was taken. It is staggering to note that companies such as General Motors and Ford have photo files consisting of several million different photos—and for good reason.

Art   There is no rule which says that publicists must confine their art techniques to photographs. The creative publicist often can enliven a news or feature story with various kinds of drawings. This is especially helpful for trade publications which usually receive an unending series of dull photographs and do not have the budgets for staff artists. "Line art" also is great for fashion and as diagrammatic accompaniments to technical photos.

Another offbeat technique is to purchase engravings or photos of nostalgic or historcal scenes from the Bettman Archive or stock photo services.

The use of color photos is extremely expensive, and, whether one provides type-C prints or transparencies, it generally should be done on a query basis or by use of one of the specialized services, which operate like the newspaper publicity mat services. Many of the newspapers which use ROP color still have poor reproduction processes, as compared to the fidelity of black and white, and publicists should carefully consider using the color services, which are likely to provide color mats or other means of enabling superior color reproduction. Major newspapers and magazines generally prefer to use their own photographers and studios for color photography, and it, therefore, is wasteful to provide them with color photographs.

Glossy prints, or glossies, are the most common form of publicity photograph, and publicists should keep in mind that these prints should have high contrast between the light and dark areas, because of the manner in which newspapers screen and reproduce photos. A high-contrast picture often produces a hard, harsh look, and a studio portrait photograph can be set up in such a way as to create a softer look, without geting into a low-contrast photo.

A publicist need not be a professional photographer, but the more he knows about photographic techniques and the reproduction of photographs by the media, the more he is likely to be able to produce and select photographs which will be used, rather than photographs which will be discarded. For example, most publicity pictures show the heads of people, but astute cropping often can be utilized to zero in on a particular feature, such as a part of the face, perhaps the eyes. You can experiment with cropping and produce photographs that are extremely artistic, amusing and, in various other ways, off the beaten track. Another advantage of cropping is to eliminate dishes or liquor glasses on the table, microphones or other items which tend to clutter up the picture.

It often is too late to attempt to do this form of editing by cropping, and the alert photographer should be on the lookout for these kinds of details at the time the picture is taken. Insist that the photographer take more than one picture, even though the photographer will tell you that he's never had a problem. Even with high-speed photography, it is possible to get a picture at the time a man is blinking his eyes, so that he appears asleep. This is particularly likely to happen in a group of people and is another reason for regrouping the people, so that they do not become impatient while the photographer takes the same scene several times. Similarly, taking the same picture several times will enable the photographer to move in closer or to photograph from different angles, so that different types of expressions can be obtained, and even to create a mood out of what would otherwise be a routine picture.

There usually isn't time to retouch the negative, and the results often are too obvious. However, in the case of publicity pictures which are utilized for booklets or other purposes, airbrushing and other types of retouching, if done by professionals, can serve to open eyes which were closed at the time of the picture, eliminate frowns and produce other miracles.

The publicist who regularly works with contact proofs finds it helpful to own a magnifying glass (an 8-power magnifier costs only a few dollars) for use in selecting and cropping photos. The extent of involvement in the photographic process sometimes is a reflection of the personal interests of the publicist. Some publicists have studied photography and are excellent photographers. This can be a profitable skill, particularly for the beginner. Whether or not you know how to operate a camera, you should know how to recognize a good publicity photo and how to help to produce it.

Filing   Always order a few more prints than needed for the initial mailing, as reorders sometimes are difficult or time consuming.

What do you do when the print supply is limited, and you need all of the prints for distribution to editors or others? Instead of merely filing the caption, the answer is to use your office copying machine to make a photocopy. Attach this to the caption, and you have a complete record. It can be extremely important in case someone subsequently wants to know exactly which picture was distributed, and it's useful for reordering photos.

Another record-keeping use of your Xerox or other copying machine is to make copies of the address labels before they are mailed. An economical way to do this is to cram as many labels or address portions of envelopes onto the copying area as possible.

DAILY NEWSPAPERS

O.K., you've written a good news release, produced a good photo and have prepared the package in an expert manner. Now, where and to whom should it be sent? Perhaps the greatest use of publicity material is by the women's departments of newspapers. In addition, the business news departments of major newspapers are big consumers of publicity material. Small-circulation newspapers frequently utilize only local business news and confine their regional and national coverage to material taken off the wires, as well as reproducing the stock tables, so that mass mailings of national business news releases to newspapers are not likely to be utilized. Of course, there are many exceptions, but, among the various departments of a newspaper, the women's section probably is the largest medium for the publicist. Furthermore, the section of the newspaper which is most likely to retain the name of the company or its products is the women's section, as women's editors frequently sanction the credits as part of "reader service."

The city editor, on the other hand, is more likely to be hard-news oriented and less receptive to commercial publicity sources. However, the role of the publicist is to work with each department, in accordance with the specific interest of the particular event or story.

Duplication On occasion, it may occur to you that more than one department may be interested in a particular news release, and the dilemma is whether to send it to one or the other or both, but to indicate that you're doing that, since there is nothing more likely to cause long-lasting trouble than to have the same news release appear in two different departments of a newspaper on the same day. You can get away with it only once or twice and then are likely to find that editors have a long memory for what

31

they feel to have been chicanery, when, in actuality, it probably merely was the result of overeagerness or, sometimes, ineptness.

Rather than try to decide which of several departments might be interested, you can send a release to more than one department, providing you indicate this, so that editors can coordinate with each other. Of course, it is chicanery to write a slight variation of the same story and send it to different departments. A more efficient procedure, in dealing with a complex story, is to separate the elements that are of interest to different departments and then to service, on the same day or at different times, the different news release to the appropriate departments.

Major newspapers frequently have reporters who cover specific industries, geographic areas or other "beats." In such cases, the proper procedure is to send the news release to the reporter who covers your special interest or other field, but also send the news release to his editor. There are several reasons for this, one of which is you never can be sure that a reporter will be in the office on that particular day.

Title vs. Individual Some publicists prefer not to send releases to editors by name, but merely by title. A more common practice is to use both the name and the title and to keep your directories up-to-date by making note of changes of individuals, as well as of publications.

Frequently, you will deal with a particular reporter who has been assigned to a specific event or story. Don't assume, however, that this is his regular beat and that all subsequent news releases should be sent to that person. However, in many cases, it is a good idea to make a note of the name of the reporter, as his name may not be in your directory, and you may want to call him on that particular story, as well as to send him subsequent material. And, after the story appears, there may be an occasion to write or call with a thank you.

Gifts or other gratuities are inappropriate, but everybody likes a thank you and a pat on the shoulder. *Thank you* are two words which are as important as *for release*. Words which should be avoided are those in which you tell an editor that he must run a particular news release because you are an advertiser or because your boss will fire you if it isn't used, or because it is the duty and the responsibility of the publication to run it because of the importance of the organization. No kidding, these are phrases that many editors report being used to them. Remember that the editor's duty and responsibility are to his employers, stockholders and readers. The publicist does render an important service to the media, but the media's obligations are not to the publicist with regard to use of publicity material.

Exclusive One way to enhance the receptivity of the editor or broadcaster to a news release is to indicate that is is *exclusive*, providing that the statement is accurate. How does one handle exclusives, without putting all of your eggs in one basket? One way is to offer a news release exclusively for a limited period of time, perhaps a few days. This is the procedure commonly followed with columnists, who require exclusives. The usual practice for the columnist or editor who rejects an exclusive offering is to inform the publicist either by returning it or by personal conversation.

Another professional use of exclusives is to send a news release exclusively to a newspaper in a city, area, region or state. Thus, a newspaper is given the exclusive within its market, which is all it is usually interested in. Some publicists have developed procedures whereby they send one variation of a story to a newspaper in a city, marked exclusive, and another variation, also marked exclusive, to the competing newspaper. This is acceptable, providing the variations are sufficiently different and can be done, for example, in the case of fashion, in which one photo is sent to one publication, and a photo of another garment is sent to another publication in the same market.

Scheduling   When to schedule an event? In many cases, a groundbreaking, check presentation, ceremonial lunch or news conference can be scheduled at the discretion of the publicist or sponsoring organization. Obviously, you're much more likely to have press coverage on a Monday morning than a Sunday afternoon. The time of the day varies in accordance with the event, but, all other things being equal, a mid-morning time is the most preferable, as it enables you to reach the evening TV shows, which require several hours to process their films, and also to reach the morning newspapers, which in most markets have greater circulations than the evening newspapers. Note, for example, that the Los Angeles Times, New York Times, Chicago Tribune and Washington Post all are morning newspapers.

As for the days of the week, Friday often is the least successful day, for a variety of reasons, one of which is that Saturday's newspapers are the thinnest and have the smallest circulations, so that an event held on Friday is less likely to appear in Saturday's newspaper. Traditionally, for example, companies, government agencies and others, when they have a choice, release bad news on a Friday afternoon, in order to take advantage of this situation, and, in show business, "bum" movies and plays ("Turkeys") often are premiered on a Friday or Saturday.

Sunday is a bad time to stage an event because of the reduced staffs at the media, but it is an ideal time to distribute news by phone, wire or in person. Many government officials know this and obtain major coverage in Monday editions of morning and afternoon newspapers by appearing on Sunday radio and television programs.

Since Mondays and Fridays are the busiest work days for most people, the three midweek days generally are preferable times for setting up press conferences and publicity events. This also provides you with the next day for follow-up, rather than having an intervening weekend.

In setting up an event, it is a good idea to check with a local convention bureau, chamber of commerce, trade association or other organization in order to find out if there are other events which already are scheduled for the same time. In the fashion industry, Ruth Findley publishes the Fashion Calendar, which is an indispensable aid to anyone setting up events in this field.

Unfortunately, there is no publication which lists forthcoming press conferences, even in New York and Washington, where frequent press conferences are a daily occurrence. However, in both cities, a call to a trade publication or a reporter who covers your field is likely to elicit some information about events which already are scheduled. Wagner International Photos in the Time-Life Building in New York maintains a calendar of forthcoming events, for free use by customers and others.

As to the competition between morning and afternoon papers, some news releases can be dated for release on the morning or afternoon of a particular day, but for most news releases the date alone is acceptable, even though the morning delivery of the mail considerably favors the afternoon newspaper. In actuality, in many cities, the afternoon newspaper often follows the morning newspaper in use of publicity, as well as other material.

Telephoning　Telephone or mail? An exasperating question, particularly when you mail a news release and then want to follow up. Obviously, it is irritating to call and ask, did you receive the release and/or do you plan to use it, especially if such a call is made at a bad time of the day, that is, in the late afternoon in the case of morning newspapers and in the morning, in the case of afternoon newspapers, because these are the times when the desk staff is the busiest.

There are times when a call can get through, and it is proper to call if you have additional information to convey or if you are checking as to whether the editor plans to send someone to attend a luncheon or to cover a particular event. Use common sense and decency and, at the same time that you try to do your job, don't be a pest.

Tip Sheet　When inviting the media to cover events, it is a good idea to use a "tip sheet" format, that is, one which provides, in succinct form, the who, what, where, when and why. The date should include the time of the day, and the place, and note, where applicable, travel instructions.

The invitation for photo coverage should be sent to the photo assignment editor in the case of newspapers and the news assignment editor in the case of radio and television stations, in addition to an invitation to the city editor or other departmental editors. The photographers and cameramen who cover events generally are in quite a hurry, so have all of your participants and props ready at the time stated in your invitation and, wherever possible, remove drinking glasses, cigarettes and anything else you may not want in the photo—before the photographers arrive.

Media Selection Do not use the same rule for all mailings, but rather consider each new release on its own merits. For example, do not send exclusives to the same publication on a continuing basis, because competing publications soon will recognize this and will retaliate for this display of favoritism. Therefore, find occasions to offer exclusives to the lesser publications on your list and, more important, look for occasions for exclusives to the mass-circulation magazines, particularly the news weeklies, as well as syndicates and wire services.

In offering exclusives to a syndicate, wire service or magazine, it is customary to wait a few days, or perhaps a week, before inquiring as to whether your offer of the exclusive is being accepted. If not, it then would be proper to offer an exclusive to another syndicate, competing wire service or magazine, or then make a mass mailing.

There are no hard rules with regard to this and there are many variations. One way, for example, is to indicate that you are offering an exclusive "advance" for a specific period of time.

Obviously, feature stories, without a specific time peg, often are more suitable to exclusive placements. Routine news releases about personnel, products and financial information should not be handled on an exclusive basis, although sometimes advance briefings are provided to publications which have long lead times. However, this is quite different from leaking the story to favorite editors.

If an editor on a publication has rejected an exclusive advance or a story idea, it generally is not considered proper to go to another editor at the same publication, unless there is a different angle. For example, it is proper, if the women's editor has rejected the story, to then offer it to the business news editor providing there is a logical basis for doing so. Certainly, if an editor within a department rejected it, it is not proper to offer it to a columnist or another editor within the same department.

The most common file at all media is the "round file," that is, the wastebasket. One can do everything right and a news release can end up in the round file. Publicity is a business with a high-volume—low-success ratio. Nevertheless, many professional publicists regularly increase their chances of having news releases thrown away. For example, large public relations departments and agencies often maintain carefully compiled media lists or utilize publicity mailing services. This is all fine except that each release really should get its own distribution list. There is a tendency to send news releases to entire lists, which not only is extravagant, but also is annoying to many of the recipients.

Publicists often justify this on the basis that editors like to keep informed. That may be true of some trade and business editors, but it is not valid for most editors and broadcasters, and it is one reason that they are turned off almost at the moment that they open most publicity envelopes.

It's very easy to irk busy editors, and publicists should try to avoid this by sending out news releases that stand some kind of chance of being of interest to the recipient. True, the cost of including a few extra names on the distribution list is relatively small. However, a release about the appointment of a branch manager rarely warrants distribution to publications outside of the branch area, except for national trade publications, and, yet, many publicity departments of large companies routinely do this. What is shocking is that these publicists sometimes are not aware that this is what they are doing, because they do not bother to prepare separate lists for each mailing.

In dating news releases, either at the top right side or as part of the first line (the dateline), it sometimes is proper to indicate an hour, particularly in the case of prereleases about speeches or other scheduled events.

In such cases, it is a good idea to telephone the media which are likely to be interested in the news release to confirm that the event has taken place and to give any changes in personnel or any other changes of the actual event as compared to the advance news release. This is an important practice, which often is ignored by publicists in connection with dinner speeches. One reason that evening TV programs and morning newspapers do not use such advances is that, in some cases, the speaker does not show up, or there are other changes and the publicist does not bother to inform the media.

Evening events present all kinds of problems, one of which is that the telephone number of the contact on the advance news release generally is an office telephone and is available only during the daytime. The careful publicist not only includes a home phone, or night line, but even can provide the telephone number at the hotel or other place at which the event is taking place.

STYLE

The preceding sections include considerable advice on the style of writing and appearance of news releases and other publicity materials. A few points bear repetition and elaboration, particularly those which are matters of opinion and personal preference. For example, many publicists devote a great deal of time to the preparation of ornate letterheads and fancy news release paper when it is the content which is far more important. Editors not only are not impressed by the color of the release paper, but often are turned off by what they feel to be something that smacks of flackery or commercialism.

The contact information, in the upper left-hand corner of the news release, should be single-spaced and occupy as few lines as possible, and appear in a discreet manner. Some publicists do not include the address but merely the phone number. This is incomplete because out-of-town media, particularly trade and business publicatons, may wish to correspond with the publicists. Always include the telephone area code with the phone number, even with releases sent only to media in the immediate area, as suburban media often have different area codes.

Down Style   The style of different publications varies with regard to capitalization. The most common style is what is called "down style," that is, a limited use of capital letters. Most titles, such as company officials, should be in small letters and should not be capitalized even though it might seem more important to the individuals involved. Some publicists feel that it is simple enough for an editor to put a lateral stroke of his pencil through capital letters in order to make them lower case. However, it is the mark of a professional to use what is the commonly accepted journalistic style, which is to capitalize only the names of publications, governmental officials and other titles, as indi-

37

cated in such standard stylebooks as those published by The New York Times or Associated Press.

A journalistic stylebook should be in every major publicity office. The sad fact is that most publicity offices have few, if any, reference books. An unabridged dictionary, a stylebook and a proofreader's symbols chart are three basic necessities, and their one-time cost is miniscule.

The corporate title of secretary can present a problem if it is not capitalized, though in context it generally is obvious that the person is a corporate officer.

Spelling   One stylistic consideration pertains to numbers. The general rule is that numbers from one to nine should be spelled out, and numerals used for larger numbers. The use of bold caps should be for acronyms and certainly should not be for trade names and other commercial words which the publicist wishes to emphasize. Abbreviations of addresses may be used, as long as one is consistent, although it is generally advisable to spell out everything in order to avoid confusion.

Business names are as important as personal names, and it is important to be careful about the various types of endings, such as Company, Incorporated, the abbreviations for these words and whether or not they are preceded by commas.

Whenever possible, simplify the company credits and omit the full name of the subsidiary or other unwieldy classifications which produce a journalistic clumsiness. For example, it sometimes is possible not to capitalize company or any part of the corporate name, and this may make the name less commercial and more palatable to the media.

On the subject of media palatability, some women prefer the Ms. title, and others object to it. When in doubt, omit the title and just use the name! What is more important is to avoid sex stereotyping in news releases and other materials. For example, it is important to get rid of job titles that suggest gender. In the process of modernizing terminology and even grammar, the publicist will find that a sensitivity to the women's liberation movement (and other social issues) can produce more colorful, euphonious and contemporary writing.

In some cases, the transition is simple, such as from salesman to sales representative, repairman to repairer and stewardess to cabin attendant. In other cases, such as the use of chairperson for chairman, the result may be awkward, and the decision is a matter of opinion.

What is not in the realm of opinion is the use of corect spelling and other matters of accuracy.

Big-city slickers often forget that a community may be a city, township, borough or other designation which should be carefully checked, particularly when identifying officials.

In the case of offbeat spellings, particulary of names (e.g. Smyth), you may call this to the attention of the editor or typesetter in a variety of ways, such as the two words, *correct spelling*, or the word, *stet* (let it stand), or the symbol cq (which means, this is correct) in parentheses or in the margin.

Another useful word is *sic*, a parenthetical insertion to call attention to something anomalous or erroneous, such as an intentional misuse of grammar or misspelling.

An experienced publicist, particularly one who works on house organs, booklets and other publications, is familiar with proofreading terms and generally has a proofreader's chart at his fingertips. Every publicist should be familiar with printer's terms, as it sometimes is necessary to make handwritten changes on previously printed news releases, and also to provide instructions to seretaries and mailing services. For example, one of the most common terms is *stet*, which can be written in the margin to indicate that a word which has been crossed out, or other editing change that has been made, should be *disregarded*, and the copy set as it was originally written.

Page Numbers   A page-numbering technique occasionally used by wire service reporters is to put at the top of the page the last word on the previous page, together with the reporter's last name and the page number. For example, if page one of a news release by Carol Deegan ends with the word, product, the leader on page two would be:

deegan/2/product

Publicists can use this technique, though a more common format simply is to put the page number at the top or bottom.

EMERGENCIES

Many books and courses deal with helping communicators with emergency situations, such as major accidents, fires, explosions. One of the most difficult roles in these hectic, emotional crises is that of the spokesperson, who often is the public relations official. Following are 10 brief reminders. This incomplete list is designed merely as a general guide. Obviously, each organization should have its own emergency procedures.

1. Don't discuss the law. Avoid discussion of responsibility, legality, liability.

2. Be complete and accurate, but

3. Don't provide unnecessary information or details. Be succinct.

4. Try to be conclusive, in order to have a minimum of callbacks and followups.

5. Stick to written, approved text; don't extemporize.

6. Speak only in behalf of the company, or organization, not in behalf of transportation carriers, customers, vendors.

7. Be as affirmative as possible; don't blame anyone; avoid judgments.

8. Do not release names of injured people until next of kin is notified.

9. Do not permit press to wander around unescorted.

10. Be calm.

WRITING

Good writing starts with proper grammar, syntax, spelling and attention to rules which often are violated by publicists (and journalists). The publicist sometimes has a different objective than the journalist, particularly with regard to presenting the client's view, mentioning the product, company or other "credit" and adhering to strictures set up by the client's legal counsel, accountant or other advisors.

In spite of this different orientation, all publicists and journalists should try to write clearly and correctly—at all times. To do this, the publicist should reread a news release after it is written and not "knock it out."

Take the time to determine if the news release (or letter or other publicity material) is accurate, clear, concise, complete and interesting. Ask these questions:

Are sentences too long, complex, cluttered?

Are words ambiguous, likely to be misspelled, mispronounced or misunderstood?

Are antecedents clear? To whom do these words refer: we, it, company, spokesperson.

Are acronymns and initials identified? Are technical terms explained?

Is the construction loose or unwieldy? Not every sentence must be succinct; rhythm flow and colorful language are important, but not at the risk of redundancy, obscurity, complexity and wordiness.

Repetition may impress the client, but publicity is not advertising. Avoid unnecessary repetitions of "commercialisms," padding, superfluous quotations.

Lucid writing is not dull. Look for active verbs, instead of passive, offbeat phrases (if clearly understood) instead of cliches

41

and colorful, descriptive words instead of hackneyed expressions.

If legalisms, foreign words, trade jargon, technical expressions and complex phrases are necessary, try to explain them. Better to use a trite or awkward expression which is understood than one which is ambiguous or difficult to comprehend.

Opinions, pejorative statements and quotations should be attributed to a person with a complete name and identification. Quotations attributed anonymously to a "spokesman for the company," or to an organization, are not advisable. If the title is cumbersome, it need not be used completely, in order to avoid roadblocks in writing. The rule is simply to avoid pretentious and mysterious writing, and anticipate questions which editors and readers may ask.

Forceful verbs, descriptive adjectives and adverbs are helpful if they enable the reader to visualize, but try to link them with precise details so that the "color words" do not appear to be exaggerative or overly subjective. Metaphors, similies, analogies and other figures of speech are fine, if they are clear in the proper context and do not interrupt the flow. Don't strain to develop colorful phrases. Try to avoid unrelated or mixed metaphors, ambiguous humor, unintentional puns and overly intellectual or sophisticated references.

Avoid sexisms, but do not go to ludicrous extremes. For example, it's proper to delete unnecessary references to gender by substituting mail carrier for mailman and similarly to use words such as police officer, executive, official, member. However, editors and publicists may not be sexist in continuing to use chairman or chairwoman instead of chairperson. It's up to you to decide if you're comfortable with spokesperson instead of spokesman. Contemporary usage also calls for a reexamination of words to describe young people. Boys, girls, youths, youngsters, children, babies and infants refer to various ages under 18. Over 18, it's men and women.

It indeed is enjoyable and enlightening to read The New York Times Manual of Style and Usage. Following are a few random comments about common errors and items which may be surprising.

A firm is a partnership and is not synonymous with corporation or company. Therefore, a p.r. firm is not the technically correct way to identify an agency which is incorporated.

Some words and phrases are commonly misused, but that does not justify our use of them. The phrase "human race" is incorrect, as the human species comprises several races. Incidentally, note that the whole comprises the parts, and the word comprise is not to be used in the reverse manner.

The general rule with regard to capitalization of academic and corporate positions is to capitalize when they are used before the name, e.g., Professor Jones, but not to capitalize when used after the name, e.g., Dr. Jones, chairman of the department of history.

Governmental positions and departments often are capitalized.

Another tricky area refers to the use of quotation marks. Book titles require quote marks, except for reference books. Play and song titles require quote marks, but not magazine titles.

Here are a few other surprises:

Henry Jones Jr.—note that there is no comma before the Jr.

April 1978—note that there is no comma! The comma is only used with a full date, such as April 27, 1978.

Dow Jones—no hyphen.

A dock is the space between piers or wharves; it is not a pier or wharf.

In the preceding sentence, note the proper use of a semicolon. Similarly, semicolons are used to separate a series of three or more commas, e.g., the committee included John Jones, president of the company; Henry Smith, vice president of the company's fertilizer division; Jane Brown, an attorney, and Jack Johnson, mayor of Centerville. Note that a comma, rather than a semicolon, is used before the last item.

The most important considerations in writing a news release are the content and literary quality. Lively, colorful, concise writing requires more care than proper use of punctuation. However, we should strive for a higher level of excellence than now generally exists. Publicity writing can be improved, and, in making it more precise and concise, rules of grammar and punctuation are extremely helpful.

DISTRIBUTION

Directories   One of the finest media directories is the Ayer Directory, which lists all of the daily, and almost all of the weekly, newspapers, and most of the trade, business and consumer publications, as well as various other categories, such as farm, college and ethnic publications. Of course, the Ayer Directory lists only the names of the publishers and/or editors, and departmental heads and other staff members are not listed. These names are listed in other directories, such as Working Press of the Nation, Editor & Publisher and several local directories, such as New York Publicity Outlets, Hudson's Washington Media and California Publicity Outlets.

Many publicists own copies of these directories and do not realize that they are gold mines of useful information. One of the advantages of Ayer, for example, is its maps and lists of counties, along with information about cities and counties. As a result, it is possible to use Ayer as an encyclopedia reference and, more important, to locate the names of publications in areas in which the publicist is not familiar.

Localizing   For example, if a news release is about an individual in a small town, consultation under the name of that town, as well as a glance at the state map, can be helpful in locating the names of every publication, particularly major daily newspapers near that town. Keep in mind that the daily and weekly newspapers in the "county seat" often print information about the entire county.

In a news release with the names of several people, a very useful technique is to append a note, or even type in at the top of the release, indicating the name of the individual or individuals who are likely to be of interest to a particular local publication. In some cases, it is helpful to add the street address or telephone number of that individual, if it is not included in the printed portion of the news release. Some offices have a rubber stamp or sticker which they append to a news release with such statements as:

> Note to Editor: There is a local angle in this news release.
> Note to Editor: This news release is being sent to you because (name) lives at (local address).

Another extremely useful technique is to append a note, or even use a rubber stamp, giving the name of the subsidiary company, office, branch store or other local data. In this way, news releases about company executives, earnings and other news releases, which might not be considered to be of local interest, are likely to be used by publications which will add the name of the company's subsidiary in their area to the news story.

It's more work to do this, but well worth the effort! One of the best ways to get extra mileage from a news release is to attribute an announcement to different people, for example, regional vice presidents or others who serve as spokesmen in their own geographical areas. Caution: make sure you send the correct fill-in to the proper publication and be sure to send the release in advance to the spokesman, so that he's not confused by a call from a local publication about a release in which he's quoted. Don't abuse this technique by providing contrived quotations which are unwieldy, awkward or inappropriate for local attribution.

And don't send more than one release to the same newspaper. Sounds foolish or impossible? A business news editor of a New York City edition reported receiving three copies of a news release. The releases were identical except for the name of the person quoted. One had a Long Island name, a second had a Westchester name, and the third had a New Jersey name—all with the same quote.

This technique can be tricky and should be used with great care and caution.

In localizing news releases, keep in mind that there are many ways in which this can be done, such as filling in the name and address of the individual, together with the title or other identification, or other types of fill-ins, such as the names of the city, state or area and data related to that locality. Because the length of the fill-in can vary, it generally is a good idea to allow for the fill-in at the end of a sentence or paragraph, so that the fill-in can be typed in without it looking obvious, and without leaving unnecessary holes. If possible, don't cram all the localized information in one place, but intersperse it in more than one place in the news release.

If the release is being sent only to local media, fill in the city, but omit the state. This is minor, but it can serve to suggest to the editor that the release is part of a national mailing. Therefore, if possible, include other local information, such as street address, number of years with the company, telephone number of local person mentioned in the release or other data—all of which can be obtained via questionnaires and set up with forms for mass processing into "holes" in a release.

Who Who should receive your news release is a question which should be asked with each news release. In the case of trade and business magazines, it generally is desirable to send it merely to the top editor and not try to address it to the departmental editor who you think would be interested, as the routing procedure is quite good at these relatively small staff publications. On the other hand, in the case of media with large staffs, such as daily newspapers, the top editor rarely is the proper person to receive the news release.

As to whether to address the news release to an individual by name or title, that is a matter of personal preference.

Some publicists claim that personnel change so rapidly that it is not necessary to try to keep up-to-date by maintaining the names of individuals. These publicists argue that all news releases are opened by the media, regardless of whether the envelope is addressed to a person by name or title, and envelopes are much more likely to be opened in the proper department if they are addressed merely by title.

The other side of the argument is presented by those publicists who claim that news releases should be directed to the proper person or persons and, though it makes the job of the publicist a bit harder to keep lists up-to-date, it can be done.

Ms. As mentioned earlier, some female editors and broadcasters have expressed preferences for being addressed with the title, Miss, Mrs. or Ms. Follow the style listed in your media directories, and be sure to add notations in your directories and lists in case of editors and broadcasters who inform you of the manner in which they prefer to be addressed. When in doubt, it might be prudent not to use Ms., as some women object to this designation.

Do not try to save a second by omitting middle names or initials, Jr. or other parts of names, as large-staff publications often have more than one person with the same last name.

Mailing Houses Here's where your typist can shortcut. In sending out publicity material to daily newspapers, radio and TV stations, it generally is not necessary to include the street address when mailing anywhere outside of the top cities. It probably also is unnecessary in the top cities, but there have been a few instances of postal clerks, particularly in New York, who have returned mail which lack street addresses. The essential ingredient in mail is the inclusion of the postal zip code, as this often speeds delivery.

In making mailings from directories, which include a post office box number plus a street address, it is advisable to address the mail only to the postal box number and certainly not to both.

Mail sent to magazines, weekly newspapers, and media other than daily newspapers and radio and TV stations, should include a street address, even in small cities.

One solution to the problem of mass mailings is to use publicity mailing services or letter shops and mailing houses which specialize in publicity. The largest company in this field is PR Aids in New York, which has many thousands of media names available to be processed within minutes.

Some publicists prefer to maintain their own lists at a mailing house or to supplement the mailer's lists with their own. When using a mailing service, be sure that your own name is on each mailing, so that you receive a checking copy, and, from time to time, request a duplicate copy of the list. The reason for this is to see exactly to whom the mailing service is sending its material and also to utilize these up-to-date lists to correct your own internal lists.

Every media directory is out-of-date and incorrect the moment it is issued, and it is the responsibility of the working publicist to keep his copy of the book up-to-date by penciling in changes and adding other material. Some publicists also use their media directories to indicate the name of editors or publications with whom they have established a telephone or personal relationship or to indicate which publications have used their material. There are all sorts of code symbols which publicists can set up to simplify this procedure. These procedures are worth the continuing effort as they enable you to prepare your own media lists quickly, efficiently and with the benefits of past experience.

There are occasions when one should send news releases or other material to the top editor of a newspaper or magazine, particularly when one is sending something that might result in an editorial, cover article or other major project.

Advertisers News releases rarely should be sent to publishers, as these individuals are more concerned with the business side of their publications. Similarly, news releases rarely should be sent to the business managers or advertising managers.

As with all publicity rules, there are exceptions. For example, a few large newspapers and radio and TV stations issue newsletters and publications which are sent as merchandising aids to local retailers and others. In such cases, it is proper to send a news release about a new product, for example, particularly when the product is being advertised in that medium, to the advertising manager or other individual in charge of issuing these kinds of merchandising bulletins. However, such news releases are not to be sent for the purpose of having them routed to the Editorial Department.

Indeed, some news releases are sent to sales or advertising managers who then note on them instructions to the news department such as "B.O. Must" (Business Office Must). It's a sore point, and generally not discussed, that some departments of newspapers, such as the Travel, Real Estate and other sections, are quite conscious of the influence of advertisers.

Quite a few trade publications, weekly newspapers, ethnic and special-interest publications strongly favor advertisers, sometimes to the total exclusion of nonadvertisers. The professional publicist must be aware of these practices and react accordingly. For example, it may be prudent simply to delete some of these publications from your mailing lists, if you are a nonadvertiser.

Another category of newspaper editor which generally should not be sent news releases is the managing editor, but this too has its exceptions as the managing editor often routes news releases to the proper department.

City Editor Releases that deal with "hard news" should be sent to the City Editor. This title varies in the case of a few major newspapers where the individual is sometimes called Metropolitan Editor.

A new title, which is being utilized at several major newspapers, is the Suburban Editor, who is in charge of editions which are distributed only in suburban areas. In most cases, suburban bureaus are under the jurisdiction of the City Editor, but sometimes are supervised by the State Editor. The State Editor, a title which is found at many major daily newspapers, particularly those such as the Des Moines Register and Tribune which have large statewide circulations, is the editor who supervises the bureaus, correspondents and part-time stringers who represent the metropolitan newspaper throughout the state. These editors often are receptive to news releases, providing there is a local angle.

It usually is wasteful and inefficient to send news releases to specific reporters, as they generally handle assignments from the City Editor, departmental editor or other supervisor. Of course, there are exceptions, such as reporters who specialize in specific subjects or who are regularly assigned to special industries, subjects or geographical areas, such as City Hall, Court House, State House.

In the case of reporters with permanent assignments of this type, as well as with top by-liners who sometimes can select their own assignments, send releases to these individuals—but *also* send the same releases to the City Editor or other supervisor, indicating that you are servicing the release in this duplicative manner. You thus are "covered," should the reporter be away due to illness, vacation or another assignment.

A major newspaper also has a Photo Assignment Editor, and, though most of these assignments are tied in with the assignment of reporters via the City Editor, occasionally it is possible to initiate a photo story via the Photo Assignment Editor.

Editors of such specialized departments as sports, women's and financial news generally operate independently of the city desk. News releases of special interest to these departments, therefore, should be sent to the appropriate editor.

At small-circulation newspapers, most of the departments are grouped under the City Editor, and there is less specialization of function. When in doubt, particularly at small-circulation newspapers, simply address the release to City Editor. The one department which is separate, in all except the very smallest-circulation newspapers, is Women's News. This department is called, "Style," "Family" or other contemporary names in a few newspapers, and those with large staffs include specialists such as Food, Fashion, Beauty and Decorating.

The Society Editor is separate from the Women's Editor at most major newspapers. Perhaps the two departments which most publicists would forever like to avoid are the Society Editor and the Obituary Writers, and this subject is discussed in the next chapter.

Letters to the Editor One section of the newspaper which is a delight is the Letters to the Editor, and surprisingly, if is often totally ignored by the publicist. This section, which has a very high readership, does not publish news releases, but does print material which is extremely laudatory and "commercial." It is possible to make mass mailings of letters, though, generally, newspapers prefer matters of local interest and also prefer to have letters which are totally exclusive or, at least, exclusive in their areas. Such letters should be addressed simply to Editor or Letters to the Editor Department. The weekly news magazines and other media also publish letters to the editor, and one should become familiar with the style of these letters, as well as their length and other considerations, which will enhance their likelihood of being printed.

Extra mileage often can be obtained from a letter to a daily newspaper by sending a copy of the letter to trade magazines or other publications which might be interested in the subject or the signer of the letter. Simply attach a note indicating that the letter was sent or was published. In some cases, a rebuttal letter or a letter-writing campaign about a controversial issue can be the subject of a news release, particularly to trade or special-interest publications.

Best Times Sunday newspapers generally publish more society items, letters-to-the-editor, feature articles (especially business features) and articles by-lined by nonstaffers than the daily editions. And, Sunday circulations are larger.

For this reason, a Sunday release date sometimes should be used, such as in announcing the name of the executive director of a nonprofit organization, as this type of news is favored by Sunday newspapers. Though large metropolitan daily newspapers often have a Sunday editor, this person generally is in charge of the various feature departments, and news for the many news sections of the Sunday edition should be addressed simply to City Editor.

Most weekly newspapers are published on Thursday or Friday, and their deadlines often are a day or two prior to their publication dates, so that news releases sent to weekly newspapers often should be mailed at different times if one desires to give the weeklies equal treatment with dailies. Publicists should know the closing dates, and time of the day, of the print and broadcast media and also the best times of the day to call. For example, the Photo Department of daily newspapers closes earlier than the News Departments, and the Feature Departments close earlier than the News Departments. Thus, the best time to call varies considerably with each department, but generally it is not a good idea to call a morning newspaper on anything except hard, fast-breaking news after 5 p.m., but rather to make the calls in the morning, when things are more leisurely. Similarly, the hectic period for evening newspapers is in the morning, and it is possible to reach these editors on the phone in the afternoon, without having the phone hung up with alacrity.

The timing of a feature news release, which is at the discretion of the publicist, is one of the few opportunities in which a publicist can try to anticipate a day when hard news is likely to be on the quiet side. Almost all publicists have their share of anecdotes (not necessarily funny, however) of carefully planned news events which have been publicity disasters because of murders, floods, accidents or other fast-breaking news events that took place at the same time.

The summer is a time when radio and television stations, daily newspapers and weekly magazines continue to operate and, in many cases, continue to have sizable audiences (in fact, radio stations often have their biggest audiences during the summer). Thus, July and August may be the best time of the year for publicists with feature articles or photos as there is less publicity activity during this season, and also the media are likely to be short of staff and more receptive to outside sources. The same strategy can be used during the last week in December or holiday weekends.

In dealing with wire services, TV stations, photo and newsfilm services, timing within minutes is extremely critical, and publicists should remember that they can deliver undeveloped, raw film to the news media. Waiting for the film developer often can mean an extra expense and a decrease in the receptivity on the part of the news media.

Mailing Tips   A publicist must know when to utilize the mail, including a recognition of the problems of postal deliveries, and when to use the telephone. Similarly, there are occasions when it is necessary to utilize messenger services, telegraph or Teletype. The alert publicist also should be familiar with a variety of other delivery systems, including the transmission of written material over telephone lines, via the facsimile systems made by Xerox, 3M, Graphic Sciences and other companies; as well as the transmission of messages via Telex.

The greatest amount of publicity material is delivered by mail. Too much, in fact, as most of it is trite, poorly prepared or not even of remote interest to the recipient. There are many ways in which publicity material can be improved. There are even a few ways in which a publicist (or other mailer) can improve mail delivery.

51

The postal situation varies considerably at different times of the year and in different parts of the country. Costs and other details may change, but some of this advice will be useful to publicists throughout the country.

1. The Post Office claims that mail deposited in the chute in hundreds of downtown locations *before 5 p.m.* is very likely to be delivered to other downtown locations in Manhattan and many other cities the following morning. This may be debatable, but, in any case, try to get out mail as it's done, in batches, rather than waiting until the end of the day.

2. The use of special delivery may be questionable. Many mailers have found that special delivery often slows up delivery, because, instead of going out on a regular morning route, it is delayed and sent via a later special route. A good solution, when sending a letter via special delivery mail, is to send a copy at the same time by regular mail.

Mail sent on Friday or the day before a holiday deserves special consideration. Is the office you are mailing to open on the weekend or holiday? If so, that may be a reason for using special delivery. However, will the person you want to receive this priority mail be at the office on the holiday or weekend? Perhaps the mail should be sent special delivery to the person's residence.

3. Mail deposited at the *General Post Office* in New York (8th Avenue and 33rd Street), before 5 p.m., will be delivered the following morning to most major cities east of the Mississippi, including Philadelphia, Washington, Pittsburgh, Chicago and Miami. It's not guaranteed, but almost. This simply is a variation of point number one and is applicable in the main postal station in other major cities.

In late 1977, the Post Office expanded its guaranteed overnight downtown-to-downtown express mail service to about 100 post offices in over 400 cities. Mailers can bring letters and packages to an Express Mail Post Office before 5 p.m., and this *guarantees* to have it at the destination Express Mail Post Office before 10 a.m. of the next business day. Guaranteed or your money back!

In 1980, the Postal Service vastly increased the Express Mail system, including many special mail boxes for pickup throughout the business areas of major cities. Over 95 percent of shipments are delivered on time, and express mail has become an important part of the publicity business.

However, private carriers vigorously compete for this business. Federal Express, for example, now has pickup carts in the lobbies of many office buildings. Purolator, United Parcel and other companies provide scrappy competition.

4. Mailgrams. This is a combination of telegram and letter, namely, copy is transmitted via Western Union and delivered by the post office the following day. It's a good idea and inexpensive compared to regular telegrams, but you have to know the postal zip code of the recipient and you must file the message at a Western Union office. These offices are few and far between,

and, in some cities and at some times of the day, it takes quite a while to reach Western Union by telephone.

Other services include priority mail for parcels, express mail and other postal innovations with which you *and* your mailers should be familiar. The U.S. Postal Service, in conjunction with its Postal Customers Council, conducts seminars for mailers at the General Post Office in New York and other major cities.

PHONE TIPS

The first minute of a phone call to a media person generally is the most important. Often it's crucial, because you may not be given more than a minute. In some cases, you may know the writer or broadcaster. In other cases, you may ask for the city desk of a newspaper, local bureau of a wire service or news department of a station and not even know the name of the person with whom you have been connected.

Plunge right in to the heart of the story. Without being curt, be brief and try to start with the purpose of your call. Don't go into an extended description of who you are. Instead, start with a headline or news lead, almost like a news announcer.

If the media person is interested, there will be ample time to fill in the details. After a brief conversation with the media person, you may be transferred to another person, perhaps a rewrite or assignment editor, or a different department.

Before the call is transferred, quickly ask the name or extension number of the person to whom you are being transferred, as the call may be disconnected or misconnected. Then, when you are connected, do not assume that the person who receives the transfer call has been briefed—start from the beginning.

Telephone calls to media people may be the most frustrating, exasperating and difficult part of publicity work. Media people *sometimes* are rude, curt, sarcastic, skeptical, arrogant. From their viewpoint, the impatience is increased when unprepared publicists call with rambling attempts to obtain publicity with weak material.

Your chance of a harmonious conversation and, more important, of a successful publicity placement is increased if you call the proper person at a logical time with a newsworthy presentation. No matter how experienced you are, you might want to literally rehearse your opening sentence, and prepare a written outline of what you want to say.

If you are not successful, don't argue or become emotional. Get off the phone, and make your next call. But before you do, try to figure out how to improve your presentation. Is it a weak story? Are you calling at deadline time? Do you have all of the necessary information?

If you are successful, be sure to button up all of the details, such as time and place of the interview or event. Then, once you've made the sale, as with all good salespeople, don't oversell, linger or overextend your welcome. Get off the phone in the same businesslike manner as you started. Now, however, you can relax!

It may be unnecessary to be reminded that calls to media people should be made by the publicist, and not by a secretary. Similarly, the publicist's office should be instructed in procedures for handling calls from media people to you. With the exception of calls from advertising solicitors, all calls from media people should be given top priority and courteous attention. A reporter can be infuriated by a switchboard operator or secretary who quizzes about the purpose of the call. The general rules of telephone courtesy, particularly with regard to not allowing any call to be left dangling "on hold" for over a minute, epecially apply to calls from media people. If you receive a call from a media person when you're not in, you, or someone else, should call back as soon as possible.

BAD AND GOOD NEWS

The Society and Obituary departments require special consideration by the publicist. One deals with good news and the other with bad news, but the assignment to send a release to either of these departments invariably is bad news for the publicist.

In some newspapers, such as The New York Times, the obit/society desk is in the same section of the city room, and there is an overlap of staffers!

Obituaries   The situation with obituaries is simpler in that this type of news is generally handled by the City Editor. Since the news must be dispatched quickly, it should be telephoned, rather than mailed. This is one of many reasons that companies and organizations should have complete and up-to-date biographies of all key people which should be readily available to the publicist for use in emergencies such as obituaries.

News releases about the appointment of executives, as well as official biographies maintained by companies and organizations of their top people, often can serve as the basis for obituaries. However, these biographies frequently omit the names of spouses and children; cities of current and former residences; occupations of parents, siblings and children; hobbies; memberships, and other personal information, all of which is pertinent and important for obituaries.

Therefore, uncomfortable as it may be, the publicist should insist that all of this information be gathered at the time the biography is prepared and an annual questionnaire be sent out to all of the individuals maintained in the corporate biography file, so that the information, particularly with regard to members of the family, but also with regard to awards and other recent information, is added to the biography. In this way, the publicist can avoid bothering the members of the family during a particularly critical time, that is, the few hours after a death, and also insure that the information is accurate, including correct spellings.

In addition, a publicist should consider sending a photo with an obituary, particularly to trade and business publications. This may seem like commercial exploitation of an extremely personal situation, but the fact is that many families of the deceased extremely appreciate this kind of attention and, in fact, often request additional clippings.

An obituary should be issued on the same day of the death. Obviously, it should not be issued prior to the death, even in the case of an accident or lingering illness. On the other hand, if circumstances are such that it is not possible to issue an obituary until a day or more after the death, the news release still should be distributed, particularly to trade and business publications.

Families often are extremely thankful for publicity which recognizes the accomplishments of the deceased person, and the publicist should do a thorough, professional job, including calls to newspapers in cities in which the subject was born, or previously lived, and mailing of news releases to trade magazines, alumni magazines and other publications. Don't ignore the broadcast media and wire services, if the subject was prominent. When appropriate, a nice gesture is to prepare a clippings scrapbook for presentation to the family. Include, when possible, previous clippings and photos and not just the obituary clippings.

The funeral director generally handles the obituary notice, which is a paid classified advertisement. However, in some cases, the publicist prepares the text of this ad and also prepares and inserts a larger "In Memoriam" ad.

More on Obituaries
Information you should have before phoning media:
1. Full name of deceased. Check spelling!
2. Birthdate, place of birth.
3. Place of youth or other places resided.
4. High school (including graduation date), college (including degrees and graduation dates).
5. Career, including most recent title, company or organization, address, highlights, awards.
6. Time and place of death, cause (optional).
7. Survivors (parents, siblings, spouse, children, grandchildren; number, names, titles if prominent.
8. Funeral (place, time) and burial.
9. Photo, if possible (professional quality, recent portrait).
10. Contact person, phone and relationship.

Bridal News
And now to the good news, which, regretfully, sometimes boomerangs into a dreary chore. Any publicist who has had a sad experience with regard to the servicing of engagement and wedding announcements to society editors can corroborate this.

Once burned, a wary publicist often tries to avoid becoming entangled in this type of publicity, as it often is extremely emotional and sensitive, and always more time-consuming than the family of the bride is aware. However, publicists often are trapped into handling this type of material, and, when they do, they should utilize the same standards of professionalism as with other publicity, including the manner in which the news release is typed and the quality of the photo.

Many publications are now using more informal pictures of the brides-to-be, and the family of the bride should be counseled with regard to this and also with regard to the retaining of a top-flight professional photographer, preferably one whose pictures regularly appear on the society pages.

Many Society Editors prefer to deal directly with the family and also to have a handwritten letter, from the mother of the bride, accompanying the news release. Therefore, even when a publicist is involved in the preparation of the material, the material should come directly from the mother of the bride or some other representative of the bride's family. Note that this is one of the rare instances in which handwriting is preferable.

The Columbus Dispatch publishes, in its women's section, the following policy in engagement and wedding news. Note the extraordinary lead times. (Obviously, hastily planned marriages cannot be publicized!)

Are You Engaged?
Here's Our Policy

The Dispatch has found it necessary to adopt the following policy on engagements and wedding news:

• The Women's Department will publish pictures with both engagement and wedding announcements if the engagement announcement and picture are at the society desk four months or more before the wedding date.

• If the time is shorter, the engaged girl may choose which announcement will be accompanied by a picture.

• Engagement pictures and announcements will not be accepted later than six weeks before the wedding.

• Bridal pictures and stories will not be accepted more than one week after the wedding. Pre-bridal wedding portraits received later than eight days before the wedding will not be considered for Sunday's edition, and the wedding story will necessarily be brief.

• Engagement and wedding forms may be obtained from The Dispatch Women's Department between 8 a.m. and 4 p.m. Monday through Friday or by sending to the department a stamped, self-addressed envelope.

- Due to space limitation, The Dispatch reserves the right to publish announcements either in the Sunday edition or during the week.

A few newspapers, including the Boston Sunday Herald American, publish "routine" engagement and wedding notices and photographs only on a paid basis. And a few newspapers follow the same practice with regard to obituaries. The Bridgeport (Conn.) Post-Telegram lists death notices at no charge, but requires advertising payment for obituary articles.

Bride's Family
The mother of the bride should use her own stationery and include her home phone number. Major Society Editors usually call to corroborate this kind of information, as pranksters sometimes send in inaccurate information with regard to engagements, weddings and deaths. Many parts of the Sunday newspaper are printed early in the week, sometimes six days before Sunday, and, therefore, Sunday's society news should be sent to the newspaper considerably in advance.

Society editors of several newspapers provide engagement and wedding announcement forms, so that readers can fill in the various details which are required with these kinds of news releases. Other publications merely advise the family to follow the format of the particular newspaper. Indeed, this format is a specialized one, in which the news generally is attributed to the parents of the bride and includes a multitude of information about the families of the bride and bridegroom.

In an attempt to get into such prestigious newspapers as The New York Times, Washington Post, Chicago Tribune, San Francisco Chronicle and Los Angeles Times, the father of the bride sometimes calls the publisher, advertising manager or others at the newspaper, or attempts to exert pressure via such intermediaries as his advertising agency and attorney. The pressures on the publicist sometimes become unbearable in such situations, particularly when dealing with egotistical families who naively believe that bribes, "contacts" and influence are the stock-in-trade of publicists.

Of course, sometimes the bride is beautiful, well-educated and has had newsworthy accomplishments of her own and then this type of assignment is a delight. As for the other type of bride (or groom), the publicist simply must grimly do the best possible job, regardless of the circumstances.

Two tips: First, if there is sufficient time, give the photo and announcement to the number-one prestigious newspaper on an exclusive advance basis. Second, deliver the material (news release, written in the style of the society page, photo and letter) in person to the Society Editor or, if not possible, by messenger.

Final tip: If possible, avoid this assignment!

PRINT MEDIA

Trade Publications Technical trade publications, professional journals and others which deal in engineering, science and other technical data are among the few media with specialized requirements, in terms of preferring lengthy news releases, sometimes even with footnotes and bibliographies, as well as accompanying documentation and other data. For such publications, it often is helpful to provide detailed fact sheets, days, or even weeks, prior to the issuance of a news release on the same subject. Many of the publications in this field, such as those published by McGraw-Hill, are extremely influential, but the publicist must be familiar with his material, so that he can be helpful to the science reporters and others at the media who can quickly spot an ill-prepared release. Therefore, publicists should consider providing technical literature and other data which is not provided to general publications. As with all media, the publicist neither should fib nor attempt to provide information about subjects with which he is not familiar, but either take the time to learn the material, or put the scientist or other technician in contact with the technical media.

One of the many advantages of publicity in technical publications is that financial analysts and others in the business community often study these publications for tips on forthcoming new products and prophecies, and other insights which are not available in the general press. In addition, reprints or articles from technical magazines often are extremely useful, because such articles tend to be longer and more authoritative than those from general publications. And, most important, technical articles often generate consumer or other publicity.

Special Audiences News releases are extremely useful for audiences other than the media, such as employees, customers, security analysts and others in the financial community, and with publics of special

61

interest to the company or organization. An extra printing of news releases often is considerably more economical than a special printing of other items, and there's something about reading a news release, particularly if it is received at the same time as the media, which gives the reader a sense of behind-the-scenes participation. Similarly, news releases, providing they are not about trivial announcements, also might be sent to stockholders and other large audiences. However, publicists should avoid adding hundreds of thousands of names to the regularly distributed news releases, as the printing and distribution costs, particularly the postage, often can amount to enormous sums of money. The conscientious practitioner should scrutinize and analyze all mailing lists on a regular basis.

As competition for space in print media and time in electronic media becomes more intense, it is obvious that the publicist must develop better materials, and rely more on personal, individual contact. However, the news release is far from outmoded or old-fashioned and remains the most commonly used form of communication between publicist and media. The majority of news releases are thrown away, but each day many hundreds of news releases are used.

A publicity mailing service recently estimated that the average investment in a news release is more than $300. This includes the cost of writing, editing, reproduction of news releases and photos, as well as distribution. Even if one ignores the editorial costs which are hard to estimate and considers only the actual out-of-pocket costs, it's still a great deal of money. Publicists who make mass mailings to hundreds or thousands of publications (which usually is totally unnecessary) frequently are not aware, or tend to forget, that these costs have become much higher than ever before, and a continuing analysis should be made in terms of comparing results with costs.

Engravings   Some weekly newspapers and trade publications have engraving charges for publicity photos. Bacon's Publicity Checker includes a notation about trade publications which have this charge as standard procedure. Major publications do not have this charge, and it is extremely annoying to receive an inquiry from a publication or, worse still, a bill, after sending them a photo. Therefore, if you do not want to authorize charges for engravings, go through your mailing lists and omit publications which regularly charge for engravings, or send them only news releases without photos.

Mats   A mat, which is the commonly used term for the matrix, or the papier-mache mold of a page of type, can be sent to weekly and small daily newspapers, providing they use the letterpress method of reproducing from the mat by casting it in type metal. Recently, many small daily and weekly newspapers have switched to photo offset reproduction, which means that they do not use linotype machines or hot metal, but rather reproduce by a photographic process. In such cases, a glossy proof, made from the mat or engraving, enables the offset newspaper to reproduce with exact fidelity.

Repro (reproduction) or enamel proofs also are called slicks. Advertisers (and publicists on occasion) often provide photos in a manner for reproduction, such as photo prints which are screened in accordance with the printing specifications. A screened print, called a velox, generally is 60 screen or coarser for newspapers. For mass mailings, a velox or repro proof costs considerably less than a mat, plastic, zinc or copper engraving, or mechanicals (from which engravings are made).

Column Size   Column widths now vary more than ever before, not just because of tabloids vs. full-sized newspapers, but also because the number of columns ranges from four to nine. A few newspapers, which have a six-column editoral format and a nine-column advertising format, use publicity mats or slicks to fill gaps in either format. The problem is further complicated by the space between columns, which means that you can't take the column width and multiply it by the number of columns. For example, here are the printing widths for a nine-column page:

    1 column .... 1 1/2 inches
    2 columns .... 3 3/16 inches
    3 columns .... 4 13/16 inches

Obviously, column widths are wider on pages with fewer columns. The most commonly used column width for publicity material currently is 1 9/16 inches for one column, 3 5/16 inches for two columns, 5 1/16 inches for three columns and 6 13/16 inches for four columns.

With this column format, there are about 32 words to a column inch. One of the most common formats is two columns by five inches. Photo captions should be about four typewritten lines.

To obtain the total size, multiply the number of columns by the depth. Thus, a two-column by five-inch format is 10 column inches.

At The New York Times, the current format is six columns of 2½ inches width for news and nine columns of 1½ inches width for display advertising. Classified ads are ten columns to a page. Display advertising space is measured in agate lines (14 agate lines to an inch), and the number of agate lines per page is 2700.

Printing Terms   The preparation of mats and offset proofs requires some knowledge of printing. This information is essential in preparing booklets and other public relations printed materials.

Though letterpress (the type of printing invented by Johannes Guttenberg in the 15th century) has been replaced by offset lithography at the majority of publications, the terminology of "hot type" letterpress still is used by printers and journalists, even for "cold type" offset.

The basic unit of measurement of type is the American point, which is about 1/72 inch. The letterpress printer obtains extra space between lines by inserting a thin strip of lead (pronounced led). The process is called leading.

An eight-point sized typeface, which is most common in newspapers, with a little extra space between the lines (that is, one extra point of leading), is indicated by 8-on-9 or 8/9. The trend is to larger-sized type and more space between lines, e.g., 9/11, for easier reading.

Hot type, that is real, three-dimensional metal type, is placed in a shallow, three-sided tray called a galley. An impression of this type thus is called a galley proof, a term which also is used for first proofs of material set with cold type. The trend is away from linotype (machines which produce hot type) to electronic production, and makeup is via pasteup, rather than lockup of metal forms.

Large publicity operations may produce their own mats or offset proofs, but a more common procedure is to make use of one of the packaged publicity services which specialize in this form of production and distribution. Though most of the publications which use this type of material are small circulation, their cumulative circulation can be extremely considerable, and, most important, those who make use of this material rarely cut it, so that the story appears complete, verbatim and with the "plug" intact. Of course, the same article can be distributed in a conventional manner to larger-circulation publications.

Another valuable function of a publicity mat service is that these companies retain several clipping bureaus, and also do a considerable amount of their own clipping and generally provide clippings as part of the fixed fee. Furthermore, the successful companies in this specialized field "service" (that is, send publicity materials to) shoppers and pennysavers (free circulation newspapers which use feature mats to fill in the spaces between ads), and other publications (some with high circulations) which are not listed in Working Press, Ayer or other directories, and otherwise are ignored by publicists.

Shoppers   A "pennysaver," which generally is half the size of a tabloid newspaper, can be a gold mine for a publicist. One clever technique is to send a collection of various sizes of "fillers" to pennysaver publishers, ranging from a few lines to several paragraphs, enabling them to plug holes with precision.

Clippings   Clippings are exceedingly important to the publicist, primarily since they are one of the few tangible evidences of success, and, more important, because the clippings can be used in reprints and circulated to prospective customers and other key groups which may have not seen the original clippings. Thus, the third-party endorsement value of an independant editor often is more valuable in its reprint form than the original audience. For this reason, print clippings, which are easier to work with than radio and TV tapes and transcripts, often are more valuable to the publicist.

Publicists generally subscribe to the basic publications in their field and read some of the publications in their geographical area, but it is not possible to read all of the publications on a mailing list. Accordingly, it generally is necessary to retain the services of a local, regional, national or specialized clipping bureau. These costs sometimes mount up into hundreds or thousands of dollars, but they are worthwhile, in spite of the lack of total efficiency on the part of the clipping bureau readers.

It not only is considered poor form, but it is a waste of time and can alienate the editor to ask him to send a tearsheet or otherwise inform you of usage of an article. An exception is the case of editors with whom you are working on some kind of exclusive basis, and it is obvious that you have invested the sufficient amount of time as to be in a position to ask such a favor.

Clipping bureaus suggest that you send them copies of all news releases, together with the names or categories of media which you are servicing, and to continually inform them of brand names and other key words that they should look for. This sometimes is helpful, though few clipping bureaus are as efficient as they claim.

Color   Publicists should constantly be on the lookout for publicity uses of materials which have been prepared for other purposes. For example, color separations often are used in the preparation of annual reports, booklets and other publications, and it often is possible to offer these color separations to trade and business publications. These editors will use them as covers or in other large, important space, partly in order to save money, but also because these color photographs frequently are quite good, since they have been prepared carefully and with the extra time which often is given to annual reports, house organs and other publications, and frequently is not given to photos taken for publicity purposes.

Clipsheet   Large publicity operations may assemble a collection of articles and photos and print them as a page or bulletin called a clipsheet, which is distributed to a large number of publications in the same manner as syndicates and wire services distribute their materials. Publications which reproduce by offest sometimes copy directly from clipsheets, while other publications will use the clipsheet as the basis for articles or to request the full articles, glossy photos or other information from the publicity source.

A clipsheet with black and white photos can indicate that some or all of the photos also are available in color and is particularly useful for the women's editors of major metropolitan newspapers which utlize ROP (run-of-press) four-color reproduction. Though ROP color is used throughout the newspaper, the greatest use of it is on women's pages, particularly for food and fashion photos.

65

In mailing clipsheets, article synopses or other "offerings," it is a good idea to include a business reply postcard. However, *never* include a business reply postcard with news releases or other "conventional" publicity mailings. And, never include a news release with an advertising order or other information which is likely to confuse or offend many editors.

The publicity departments of some advertising agencies may do this, and there is no question that it works at some publications, but the professional publicist simply should avoid this practice.

The inclusion of reply postcards with scripts, tape and films sent to radio and TV stations is a common, acceptable practice, particularly with the smaller stations.

Magazines The procedure in dealing with mass-circulation, business and consumer magazines is considerably different from working with the daily media, that is, newspapers, radio and television stations. News releases can be sent to magazines, but they generally must be supplemented with personal communication. A short letter, in essence a query, to a magazine editor should outline the reason you think the publication should assign a staff or free-lance writer to do a particular article. Accompanying material may be included, but it usually is unnecessary to write the entire article. Of course, in some cases, you can work with free-lance writers, who do write the entire article. The usual process with a free-lance writer starts with the same type of inquiry letter.

Keep in mind that magazine editors scan their mail in the same way that newspaper editors do, and, therefore, a letter should be as concise and attention-getting as a news release. Unless you know the editor, it usually is not a good idea to telephone and, even when there is a telephone call or meeting, it is important to follow up with a letter.

Many editors answer mail simply by throwing it away, which is their way of rejecting it. This is frustrating to the publicist, particularly when offering a guest for a radio or television program. The use of the telephone is recommended with the broadcast media and is discussed in a later section.

A major magazine or network television program often will insist that the guest or story be exclusive. If the editor asks you about this, of course, you must be honest. It may not be necessary for you to indicate whether or not you are in the process of *querying* other media. However, it can be extremely detrimental if you break a story via the daily radio, television or newspaper media at the same time you are working with a long-lead magazine. Therefore, either start considerably in advance with the magazine editor or else be prepared to work with magazines on subjects which are totally different from those with which you are working with the other media.

Free Lancers One advantage of querying editors of mass-circulation magazines and free-lance magazine writers is that it is possible to send out a large number of queries at the same time. Those which respond to the queries then can be provided with different aspects of the articles, or the publicist can be in a position of selecting which of those who respond should be given first crack or exclusive rights to the story.

Many magazines prefer to purchase material from free-lance writers, rather than deal with publicists, as they then can rely on the integrity of the free-lance writer to provide material which is not only exclusive, but has been carefully researched with regard to its accuracy and "down-keyed" with regard to its commercialism.

Thus, a publicicist often will deal with a free-lance writer. By studying the by-lines in the magazines, one is familiar with the names of free-lance writers who regularly write for these publications. The names of many of these writers can be found in Working Press. In addition, one can obtain the roster of various organizations, such as the Society of Magazine Writers.

It is not ethical to pay a free-lance writer who is also paid by the media. In some cases, it is possible to retain a free-lance writer who then will inform the magazine that he is working for you and is willing to accept a reduced payment or no payment at all. Free-lance writers also are available to write booklets, speeches and other items, and, in so doing, become sufficiently interested in the subject that, on their own, will query magazines and, thus, often are more successful in placing articles than publicists. The free-lance writer not only is a professional writer, but also is intimately familiar with the up-to-the-minute requirements of the media with which he regularly works.

It is a good idea to read publications such as The Writer, Writer's Market and Party Line, in order to keep up-to-date on the needs of the media, and also on articles that free-lance writers and magazine staff writers are contemplating or already are researching, so that one can send them material. In such cases, the recommended approach is via telephone as by the time the tip appears in these publications, it usually is in the final stages.

Magazine publicity can be extremely influential, and it is worth the time to prepare a synopsis, work with free-lance writers and engage in the various time-consuming techniques that are more elaborate than the preparation and distribution of news releases to newspapers. Of course, it is possible for an article to appear in a magazine which is exactly as you prepared it with only one change and that is the deletion of the company or product name. On the other hand, it is possible to deal with magazine departmental editors and columnists in the same way as in newspapers. For example, the women's, business and other magazines, such as the news weeklies, have departmental editors with special interests, so that one can send them news releases and product photos in much the same way as with newspapers.

In addition to news releases, publicists should consider the possibility of fact sheets or other material sent as background information on a periodic basis. In such cases, it sometimes is proper to include an annual report, booklet or even catalog sheets, even though they are commercial. These materials are particularly useful with trade publications.

Case Histories An important technique in working with trade and business publications is the preparation of detailed case histories, which are sometimes written in the form of a by-lined article by an executive, scientist or other representative of the company or organization. In other cases, a case history can be an elaborate fact sheet which is provided to the trade or business editor to enable him to prepare a more complete article.

Some publications, such as the Fairchild newspapers, prefer to work directly with the source and try to shun publicists. The procedure varies with each publication, and some of the major media issue booklets and guidelines to publicists. For example, the McGraw-Hill publications are extremely helpful to publicists and provide booklets with tips on writing for their specific publications. The best way to know the publication is to read it and study it.

Interviews A major goal of the publicist often is to set up an interview. This is accomplished by a letter, phone call or visit. Once the interview is set up, the job of the publicist is far from over.

First, confirm the time and place of the interviewer and interviewee.

Second, make sure that the interviewee is briefed about what you discussed with the interviewer and that the interviewee has copies of all news releases and background material which might be needed.

Third, make sure the interviewee arrives on time. Provide travel directions, including room number, and, if necessary, arrange for transportation.

Fourth, try to avoid telephone interruptions or other distractions. If the interview is in the office, try to "cut off" the phone. If the setting is a restaurant, select a quiet place which does not have elbow-to-elbow seating.

Finally, decide whether or not you should be present. Certainly it is obvious that the interviewer should not be surrounded by more than one publicist, and, in some cases, the publicist should not be present at all.

To repeat: before the interview, brief the interviewee. No matter how experienced the person, do not assume that the preceding and following advice is redundant.

Nothing is off the record. An interview often resembles an informal conversation, and the interviewee may be tempted to make wisecracks, criticisms of competitors or other remarks which can be embarrassing when they appear in print. It is not a matter of trusting the reporter, but a fact of life that people remember secrets more than something which is "on the record." The best way to protect yourself, and not to confuse the reporter, is simply not to go into any discussions which are private.

An interview is not a court trial, and the interviewee is not required to answer every question. If you do not wish to discuss income or other confidential data, simply state that the information is not available. Whenever possible, try *not* to be interviewed over the telephone. Of course, there may be times when a reporter will ask a simple question, particularly if it is after an in-person interview, and you certainly should reply on the phone. In other cases, a telephone question leads to a discussion, and you should try to conduct the discussion in person.

Remember that a telephone conversation is on the record. Do not be trapped by a magazine writer or reporter who is requesting information for a *potential* article or any other technique which is designed to provoke opinions or comments which may turn up in print in a way that is potentially embarrassing. A phone conversation or personal interview may be recorded. In some cases, you may not be informed of this.

TV INTERVIEW TIPS

Try to be so well prepared that you don't need to bring notes with you. If you are promoting a magazine, book or product, bring it, of course, but as a "visual" and not to read from it.

Sit in the interviewee's chair before the TV show begins, in order to get accustomed to it. Relax. Stay in the chair during commercial breaks and after the program ends—until the host or producer tells you that it's over.

Walk around to relax, but don't touch TV equipment.

Provide the producer with slides, boards or other visuals. If you plan to display the product or use other props, inform the producer and mutually agree where to place the items and how to show them.

If you are a novice, get a professional to videotape a rehearsal and advise you about style and content. For example, try to avoid rapid head and body movements. Do you perspire noticeably? Do you roll your eyes upward when answering a question? Do you grimace? Do you stare into space when others are speaking? Do you blink excessively? ... A professional communicator can help you!

If you are involved in a controversial issue or adversary situation, be prepared with answers for all types of questions, particularly how to defuse "loaded questions."

Keep calm! Know when to be brief and when to elaborate. Listen carefully. Try to be positive, accurate, nonevasive. Remind yourself which answers you want to convey, and work in these key points—in some cases, regardless or in spite of the questions.

SPECIAL EVENTS

The setting up of a news conference, luncheon fashion show or other special event to which the press is being invited, requires elaborate, time-consuming preparations by the publicist. Company executives and others who work with the publicist rarely recognize the amount of attention which must be paid to this difficult task. The procedure varies in accordance with the event, but following are a few tips to serve as a general checklist.

Invitations A solution to the thorny problem of when to send out an invitation to an event is to send two invitations, the first considerably in advance of the event, that is, about two or three weeks prior to the event, and the second, often with late news or more detailed information, a couple of days prior to the event. With regard to the last-minute invitation, don't forget to allow an extra day or two for the occasional postal delays, as well as for the fact that the recipient may not be in the office every day.

PR Newswire Another solution to the matter of proper timing of invitations is to send one invitation by mail and then follow up a day or two prior to the event by using one of the publicity Teletype services, such as PR Newswire. If nothing else, the private newswire ensures same-day delivery, and, though the cost is about $70 per usage, which is more than most mailings, it is an amazingly efficient procedure. There are many instances in which a mailed news release is ignored or lost, but the same material, on the newswire, receives immediate attention. Editors increasingly understand the difference between the publicity newswire and their own news Teletype services, but somehow the use of the newswire indicates that you have taken the extra trouble, and perhaps moves up the event a notch in importance. In many cases, television news teams and newspaper photographers arrive at events with the tip sheet torn off the PR Newswire or other news Teletype services. A telegram might have the same effect, except that Western Union cannot guarantee same-day delivery, and, in many cases, telegrams are telephoned to the recipient, rather than delivered.

Special events require a knowledge of banquet catering and the solution to numerous logistical problems, in addition to the handling of the publicity function under what often are bizarre or adverse conditions. To the extent that it is possible, careful planning and adequate personnel can help to alleviate some of the pressures.

Sign-In A receptionist should be seated at a table just outside or inside the entrance to the room, preferably with a list of invitees so that they can be checked off, and then it is not necessary to have a sign-in book. In other cases, a sign-in book should be provided. An elaborate book is not necessary, and a notebook or legal pad is sufficient. The receptionist generally should provide the guests with the press kit or other materials, and the publicist should be nearby in order to greet the press.

At luncheons or other events in which the audience is sizable and does not consist solely of the press, a special table for the press can be set up. The publicist should weigh the dual consideration of setting up the press table adjacent to or near the speaker's table, so that the press can hear the speeches accurately, which may be the preference of the press, or to have their table near the door so that they can leave unobtrusively prior to the ending of the event.

Speeches Speakers at the event should be solicited well in advance for advance copies, either complete texts or summaries, which should be provided to the press as part of the kit. In the case of scientific and technical meetings, an important task of the publicist is to review papers and speeches, and not only provide summaries, but also interpretations and other background materials.

Photos and biographies of the speakers should be provided, where relevant. In some cases, an economical and efficient procedure is to have a variety of photos available, but not include them in all press kits.

When you have your own photographer at the meeting, a good idea is to inform the press, particularly those from trade and business publications which do not have fast-breaking deadlines, that you can provide them with photographs subsequent to the meeting. In the case of reporters with fast-breaking deadlines, it sometimes is possible to give them the film directly from the photographer, even though it is not developed, or to make arrangements to get them the film shortly after the meeting.

Advance The question often is asked about whether the sending of an advance news release, or the complete press kit, prior to the meeting discourages attendance. This may be so, but if the sending of the advance material helps to get it published, then the fact that there is a sparse attendance at the meeting—but there is good coverage—certainly is more important.

The matter of sending out material prior to the event is almost a necessity in the case of dinner and other evening meetings, and, in such cases, it often is a good idea to service the morning newspapers with complete material on the morning of the meeting and then to call in during the meeting in order to confirm what took place. In other cases, it is helpful to call the morning newspaper during the afternoon, that is, prior to the evening meeting, in order to establish their interest and to find out who is the proper person to call during the evening.

The alert publicist should be sure to get the names of all reporters and photographers who attend the meeting, as it is not sufficient merely to know the name of the publication or station, since the reporter or photographer may leave prior to the end of the meeting, and you may want to telephone the specific person.

Site   One rarely is able to set up a meeting with ideal conditions, but certainly those which are set up in hotels should be done in such a way that free telephones are available to the press, particularly in the case of speeches or other news-making events which will be telephoned into the media. In the case of sites which do not have free telephones, publicists should at least know where telephones are available, so that the media can be properly directed. Publicists should make sure that they not only have a supply of paper, index cards, pens and other materials for the press, but also that they have their own supply of dimes in order to make a variety of pay-telephone calls. For example, it sometimes is possible to call the media at the beginning of an event and entice them to cover by telling them what is going on. In some cases, the publicist serves as a reporter by calling in newsworthy quotes or other details and, thus, is successful even with editors who previously had not been interested in the event.

Pay phone booths often lack telephone directories, and it saves time and annoyance to be prepared with a media telephone list. A good example of advance preparation on a high professional level is a list of people with their direct dial telephone numbers and the night lines of those media (for example, the Fairchild publications) which have different phone numbers in the evening and on weekends.

In setting up news conferences or other events to which the media are to be invited, try to avoid private or chartered clubs and halls which sometimes have restrictions with regard to the media. For example, the Harvard Club in New York is a prestigious place for a meeting but will not allow newspaper photographers and TV crews to attend meetings in its building. Similarly, one can rent a rehearsal hall or meeting room in Carnegie Hall and find that union regulations forbid television cameramen from entering these premises, unless prior clearance has been obtained from management.

Check out the place that you are planning to use with regard to electric outlets, even though television crews often do not require these. Obviously, events set up outdoors require other forms of preparation, such as inquiry about the availability of restrooms and telephones in the area.

A useful service for an event, though not necessary, is a line drop, which can be a 25-amp, 120 volt outlet. Many TV stations now use minicams and often have their own vehicles or power supply. However, a publicist should prepare for a major event in every way to enhance usefulness to media people. Wall outlets generally are adequate, but should be checked prior to the event to make sure that appliances or other items are not on the same circuit. Before the event, tell the house electrician that TV crews may be plugging in their lights. As a final precaution, find out where the fuses or circuit breakers are located!

In the same way that it is possible to have your own photographer service material to the media, one may make arrangements for audio and videotaping for servicing to radio and television stations. However, the use of these commercial services is considerably more expensive than with still photographers, and one not only should carefully plan the cost of such production, but consider the cost of prints and distribution, which can total many hundreds of dollars.

RADIO AND TELEVISION

Many broadcasters, including news directors of major TV stations, look to the print media for guidance. Spectacular results often can be attained by calling the attention of a news director or talk show producer to an item in a major newspaper or magazine and suggesting an interview or feature follow-up.

It usually is wasteful to send news releases to the anchor men or individual news reporters, as assignments are made by the news director or, in the case of large radio and TV stations, by a counterpart to the newspaper city editor who has the title of News Assignment Editor.

Telephone The broadcast media, that is, radio and television stations, are more telephone-oriented than they are to letters. Thus, it often is possible to place a guest on a radio or television interview program by means of a telephone call. The person to call may be the interviewer, producer or a person whose sole function is to book the guests. The credits broadcast at the end of the program may provide these names, but the publicist who regularly works with these programs should purchase one or more of the directories and services produced primarily for this purpose.

Even the most self-confident publicist often hesitates to call an editor or broadcaster who has been known to be brisk with calls from publicists. Thus, the perennial question, to call or not to call, is difficult to answer. Even in this time of commonly used long-distance calls, it is a fact that a person-to-person long distance call is much more likely to get through to almost anyone than a local call to the same person.

Who to Call A national directory, such as TV Publicity Outlets, is essential to anyone who regularly attempts to book guests on programs. If you do not have a directory, and also to obtain up-to-the-minute programming information, you sometimes may call the program or news director for guidance. Outline the subject, time availability and name of guest as briefly as possible, and ask whom should be contacted at the station.

An offbeat aid is the magazine, TV Guide. Write to TV Guide in Radnor, Pennsylvania 19088, for a current copy of the local edition in each market in which you seek publicity. The listings often provide program information not found in directories, as well as station and personality details which may be useful to the publicist or the interviewee.

When you have arranged for a guest to be on a local program, you may want to obtain the local edition of TV Guide and local TV newspaper supplements on the chance that your interview is listed. When TV interviews are arranged sufficiently in advance, this type of print publicity can be enhanced by sending photos of the guest to the publicity director of the TV station.

Exclusives   Major programs sometimes require exclusives for guest interviews. The exclusive may mean that the guest cannot appear on any other program on that station for a week (or two) before the interview. The rule at radio station WOR in New York is 13 days. This is extraordinary, however, and the rule sometimes is waived for prominent guests or other reasons.

The exclusive may refer to all other radio and/or TV programs in the city or market. In a city with two major live interview programs, the choice often must be made between a morning and noon TV program, each of which requires exclusives.

The program producer or guest coordinator sometimes assumes that the experienced publicist is familiar with the policy with regard to exlusives. If the subject is not discussed, the publicist may be in a quandry. If you ask the program, you may be told about exclusivity. If you don't ask, you may "get away with it." However, the question of exclusivity may be raised the day before the interview. In order to avert a last-minute cancellation or other "wrath," it's better to bring up the question in advance. However, with print media, it's not necessary to inquire about exclusives, though a few competitive newspapers do require exclusive interviews.

Time of Day   Because of the time difference, publicists in the Eastern zone can make profitable use of their time at the end of the day by calling major editors and broadcasters in the Western part of the country. The trick is to know whom to call, when to call and, most important, what to say. A good reason for a phone call is to offer the editor or broadcaster a person to interview or to provide information that has not been included in a news release, or to suggest a specific exclusive story or interview.

When telephoning any editor or broadcaster, be sure to have your notes in front of you, know your subject, and compose your thoughts in a way to make your call concise and successful. Obvious advice, but often blatantly ignored. The chit-chatty small-talk offenders range from the naive to the most experienced.

The call should be followed up with written material, even if the letter merely confirms the time at which the person will be interviewed.

The radio and television people who book guests tend to be more harassed at certain times of the day, and this is not necessarily the time when the program is about to go on the air, as many programs are taped. It is a good idea to know when is the best time to call, and this varies considerably among different programs. Generally, radio and television people, as is customary in show business, arrive later in the morning and tend to work in the evening hours, and it often is possible to telephone quite late into the evening from the East and reach West Coast radio and television programs.

In the case of radio news and interview programs, it is not necessary for the guest to go to the station, or even to be in the same city, as recorded telephone interviews often are the preferred technique. Considerable broadcast exposure can be obtained in this manner, without the time and expense of travel. (And, of course, newspapers and other print media do telephone interviews.)

Confirmation Immediately after a journalist or broadcaster agrees to interview your client, send a confirming letter or memo to the interviewer, with a copy to the interviewee. Be sure to include, so that there can be no misunderstanding or confusion, the day, date, time (a.m. or p.m.), number of people who will be there (i.e., will you and/or others accompany the interviewee), place and exact address (e.g., dining room on main floor of hotel, not coffee shop on lower level).

If a restaurant reservation is required, make it immediately, and don't wait until the day of the interview. You then may find that the restaurant is closed that day, and it may be too late to inform the interviewer or interviewee. If you make the reservation in the name of the interviewee, add this information in the confirming note.

Tour Schedule In addition to a thorough briefing, interviewees who are sent "on tour" should be given a separate folder for each city with the itinerary for each day itemized in an easy-to-read format.

The itinerary should include whom to contact, where and when, and a variety of useful information, such as when to eat and distance between appointments. Don't assume that the interviewee or the taxicab driver knows the location of a TV station, particularly since a program may be taped or broadcast from a location which is across the street or miles away from the station's offices.

Video Material The simplest and cheapest video material is a photograph. A script or news release can be accompanied by one or more photos, and it's often useful to have an interview guest with photos, as well as products, models, charts, maps and other props. Photographs for television should be matte-finish, not glossy, and mounted on 11 x 14-inch or larger cardboard, called a ballop card, or glass-mounted (not cardboard) on 35mm slides. Whenever possible, photos and film should be color. Large photo blowups can be dramatic backdrops.

Television film is 16mm, not eight mm, which is associated with home movies, or 35mm, which is used in theaters. 35mm film can be converted, and eight mm film can be used by some stations, but it rarely is.

Videotape should be two-inch, high-band tape, though one-inch tape often is acceptable. Home videotape units generally use ¼-inch or ½-inch, and this cannot be used by TV stations.

Publicists who are amateur photographers have an advantage in knowing about lighting, composition and other ways to improve picture quality. However, a professional photographer should be retained for all motion pictures and almost all still photography.

Audio Materials Electrical transcriptions (ETs), a type of recorded disc, no longer are used on radio stations. Records of music and interviews, of any standard speed, including 78 rpm, and size, including small discs, are common, though tape is used more often by publicists. Any standard speed tape is acceptable (be sure to mark the speed on the box and the reel), though the most common is 7½-inch (speed) full-track, ¼-inch (width) tape. AM and FM stations can use this, and thus it is not necessary to produce stereo tape for the stereo FM stations. Tapes can be on reels or cassettes.

PSA's An economical "mass-distribution" broadcast technique is the public-service announcement which is utilized by many non-profit organizations. These announcements, which are provided in the form of audio or videotapes, cartridges or films, should run a specified length, such as 20, 30, or 60 seconds, and the time should be carefully indicated with the accompanying scripts.

In writing copy exclusively for radio and television, keep in mind that this type of journalism is quite different from the print media and involves shorter sentences, with fewer ideas and facts in each sentence. A 10-second announcement might consist of about 25 words on radio and only about 20 on television, so that a one-minute news report or public-service announcement runs to only about 150 words on radio and less on television. This means that you have to compress your ideas and cannot be as expansive as you might in a news release. Of course, leisurely writing usually doesn't do well even in a news release, but, in any case, try to write your radio and television copy in a way in which one idea is confined to each sentence or phrase, without making the writing dull or overly elementary. The broadcast style is more conversational and informal and, for example, you're much more likely to use vernacular words and contractions, but try to do it without getting sloppy.

Public-service announcements must be in behalf of nonprofit organizations. Most stations will not permit announcements about bingo parties, lotteries or events of this type.

PSA scripts (and other scripts for radio and TV stations) should have wider margins than news releases, start lower down on the page and may be typed triple-spaced instead of double-spaced.

The top of the script should include the number of words, approximate time for events and specific dates when the material can be used, such as, "Use between Monday, July 1, and Saturday, July 6."

It's also helpful to send each station several extra copies of the script.

A more detailed discussion of public-service announcements appears in the next chapter.

Scripts Small and medium-sized TV stations are major users of slides and films provided free to them by publicists.

If you are going to take the time and spend the money to provide audio and/or visual materials, don't try to short cut by using news releases or other print media materials. Radio and television scripts must be short, relatively simple and written to be spoken. Avoid abbreviations, long and hard-to-pronounce words and cumbersome phrases. After you write the script, read it aloud.

Sentences must be short and punctuated to allow for pauses. Avoid parenthesis marks or other symbols which present problems for the announcer or listener. Avoid clauses, even when they are set off by dashes or commas, as they are likely to be ignored by the announcer or misunderstood by the listener. For example, a news release might state, John Brown, mayor of Middletown, . . .

The script version would be, Middletown Mayor John Brown.

In order to make it as easy as possible for the announcer to read and broadcast your script, spell out all numbers (you may wish to insert the numerical figure in parentheses), and insert in parentheses the phonetic spelling or pronunciation of names, foreign, difficult or unusual words. You may wish to triple-space the script and use wide margins.

Brevity is essential in scripts, but clarity is of greater importance, so, if necessary, repeat the information, in a slightly revised manner, in accordance with the broadcasting adage "First, you tell them you're going to tell them; then you tell them, and then you tell them you told them."

Many newscasters start with a "billboard" or "tease," which gives the highlights, somewhat like a headline, then follow with the item, and conclude with a "wrap-up" or summary.

16mm films, preferably produced in color, may be distributed in silent or sound versions, accompanied by a script, in various lengths. Since most of these feature films are used on local news programs, the length should be kept brief, such as one minute.

Be sure to indicate the exact time of the film at the top of the script, as well as the length of each scene.

Slides   TV slide features are more economical to produce and are widely used. The general procedure is to offer films or slides to the news program director of the station, though a few distributors provide the materials without a query letter.

For a one-minute TV slide feature, the most common package consists of four to six slides. Each slide should be numbered and identified on the frame and also described in the scripts.

Because of the many aspects of production expertise which are required with audio/visual material, it is preferable to utilize a publicity service which specializes in the production and distribution of slides, films and other materials for use by radio and TV stations. Publicists who prefer to produce their own materials should strive for professional quality, particularly the best possible photography. For example, the slides should have the subjects in the center, with the edges blank or relatively unimportant. The pictures generally should be horizontal to fill the television screen and should be sent in the form of 35mm slides, rather than mounted prints. The blankness of the peripheral areas allows the station to crop, and this applies as well to still photos sent to print media, so keep the "cutoff" area blank or with nonessential material.

Of course, it is not essential to use photos, and drawings or other artwork occasionally result in a good change of pace.

Whenever possible, convert photos or art to slides, and this may give you a chance to crop a vertical and change it to a horizontal. A television screen is about four units wide as compared to three units high, so this gives you an idea of the preferred dimensions of a horizontal slide.

The accompanying script should have about 120 words, if it is to be a 60-second length. Thus, if there are six slides, the commentary accompanying each of the slides should consist of about 20 words. A longer number of words can be used if there are less slides, but keep in mind that copy should not be too long. There generally should be some kind of introduction or lead-in to the first slide and also allowance of a few seconds for the viewer to perceive the visual material. It is also helpful to have transitional phrases between each slide.

Some scriptwriters keep their scripts even shorter, and then include a section of quips, facts and assorted material for the broadcasters to select according to their own styles. Another novel technique, and one which is an easy-to-perform service, is to enclose two copies of the script, one for the announcer and the other for the control room.

The slide package consists of a cover letter, script (one or two copies), slides (preferably inserted in sequence in a sheet or box) and return postcard. The film package consists of a cover letter, script (sometimes omitted, but a useful component), film and return postcard. Films may be sent at special postal rates, with first-class letters affixed to the outside of the package. Try not to send letters separately from the films, and be especially careful about addressing to the proper person, as this material is quite valuable.

Length   The preferred length of a half-hour film is 28½ minutes, though the time can range from 26 to 29 minutes. The 29-minute maximum is not recommended for commercial TV stations.

One-minute films or other news shorts generally are not returned. Longer feature films (a good length is three minutes) and programs (often 12 or 13 minutes, to allow for commercials to fill out a 15-minute segment) are returned and should be sent in film containers, with preprinted return mailing labels.

Slides are rarely returned, but it is permissable to request it. More important, enclose a return postcard, so that the broadcaster can inform you of the time and date of usage, together with comments or requests. If you distribute feature films or slide packages on a regular basis, you certainly should maintain a list of stations which use your material, so that over a period of time you can service only these stations on an exclusive-in-each-market basis.

The matter of audio and visual credits in films, tapes and slides must be handled with absolute discretion, as the station is more likely to discard material which is over-commercial, rather than attempt to edit it. In making films, carefully check the various methods of production; in general you'll find that the difference in cost between color and black and white, and between silent and sound, is relatively small in comparison to the total investment, and, therefore, it is preferable to produce color, sound films.

Films   Mass mailings to radio stations are handled in somewhat the same manner as TV slide films. The radio package consists of a cover letter, script (with time notation), return postcard and, whenever possible, tape or record. Many stations prefer cartridges instead of tape reels, and public-service announcements often are stacked in cartridge racks ("cart players") and used in sequence. The cartridge is somewhat like a newspaper mat; it serves as a time filler, instead of a space filler, and often is broadcast many times, with the determination one of availability rather than content. Don't put more than four spots on each disc or tape, as most stations don't bother to go beyond the fourth cut or band.

In working with the radio and television media, keep in mind that they generally are not interested in speeches, which among television people are referred to as "talking heads," but rather in action. Thus, in inviting radio and television news people to cover events, be sure to indicate items that are likely to be of interest to them. In so doing, it is not necessary to write in their technical jargon, but it is a good idea to be familiar with it and to use this terminology in the preparation of radio and television scripts that are used for public-service announcements or for other purposes.

Among the most common terms are:

LS—long shot

MS—medium shot

CU—close up

fade in, fade out

The action that takes place with the camera in one position is called a scene and the entire recording is done in takes, with each take consisting of several scenes. It is interesting to note that the word, take, which is a sequence, emanates from newspaper jargon.

A basic film glossary appears in the appendix.

Assignments   Two other carryovers from the newspaper medium which are important to the publicist are the "Day Book" and "Feeds."

The Day Book is the list of assignments for each reporter maintained by an editor. In the case of a TV station, the news assignment editor generally prepares the daily list on a sheet of paper, not a book, the preceding night or early in the day. The publicist thus must learn when to contact the assignment editor, particularly in the case of large stations, which have day, night, and weekend assignment editors.

Feeds   A feed is a series of network or syndicated films which are sent via AT&T lines by the national and regional networks and television services to local stations. The feed generally is in the afternoon for broadcast use later in the day or the following day. Thus, the contact with feed originators must be made much earlier than with live news, and generally is well suited for feature publicity, rather than "hard news."

Interviews   In working with the television medium, keep in mind that visual material will help you to make placements, and also to get across your commercial message. Therefore, be sure to have available samples of products, banners, photographs, costumes and other props. Photos or other material should be printed on non-glossy paper and mounted on cardboard, if possible. When providing guests for television programs, these visual materials should be given to the television production people at the time of the rehearsal or pre-interview, so that they can integrate them into the script. It generally is too late for the guest to bring these items with him at the time of the interview, but even this possibility should not be ignored. Many major radio and TV interview programs are planned minutes before air time.

Rehearsal   The professional publicist should rehearse with the guest and not assume that he is experienced even if he already has been on other radio or television programs. A rehearsal can consist of posing questions which the interviewer is likely to ask. In so doing, the guest and the publicist can think through how to make the answers interesting, cogent and also helpful to the publicity source.

Before any interview, particularly a broadcast interview, the publicist and the guest should decide what they want to say and

82

how to say it. A typical broadcast interview lasts only a few minutes, so it's important not to waste precious seconds. A rehearsal will not dampen spontaneity and is likely to eliminate pauses, providing the interviewee uses colloquial language and does not sound like a stilted replay of a memorized script.

Most interviewers do not want a monosyllabic guest, nor do they want one who's too long-winded. As to what the guest should wear, it is a good idea to stay away from white shirts or other white items. TV cameras tend to pick up the light from white, and on the television screens they appear dazzling. Even with today's refined equipment, and though many TV receivers now are in color, the use of white should be avoided. Of course, the traditional blue does not have to be the only color, though it still is excellent for television purposes. One color which should be avoided by women is dark red, as it may appear as black on the television screen.

It is not necessary for the guest to apply his own makeup, and some programs no longer use makeup for guests. However, the experienced television guest is familiar with the way that he photographs and often applies some kind of makeup in order to give a better coloring or smoothness to his skin. The use of the type of jewelery which is likely to be reflective also should be avoided. Men should be instructed to check the length of their socks, so that when they are shown seated on television panel programs, their pants cuffs will not reveal what could be construed as sloppiness.

Publicists should insist on briefing guests prior to appearance, even when the guest is an experienced author or official of a major company or organization. The practice session might include the use of a stopwatch or clock, as the guest sometimes is not aware of how long or short his answers take. The answer generally should be about 30 seconds, so that the interviewer and guest can have a conversation, rather than a monologue.

It is amazing to note the number of interviewers who have a minimum of preparation prior to the beginning of the radio or television program, and it, therefore, behooves the guest, and the publicist, to make up for this lack of preparation. This rehearsal is likely to produce a more interesting program and also be of greater benefit to the publicity source.

It is assumed that the guest knows his material well enough that he does not have to bring notes or other source material. If he must bring papers with him, they should be typed in such a way that they can be read at a distance (preferably without glasses) and be set up so that sentences do not break between pages. In using such papers, the guest should try to set them up unobtrusively and not rustle them when moving.

Obviously, it is preferable that the guest look up rather than read. More important, the guest should look at the camera, rather than the interviewer, or alternate his look at these two, so that he's not photographed constantly in profile.

All of this comes with experience, but the publicist is the one who is expected to have the experience. The professional publicist should review all of these matters with the guest in such a way as not to make him apprehensive, but rather to enable him to take maximum advantage of the radio or television interview. For example, the briefing should include such hints as: what to do when it is necessary to sneeze or cough during a live interview. The answer is to do the same as professional broadcasters and this is to quietly move your head as far away from the microphone as you can.

The experienced television guest knows that a monitor often is placed off to the side of the stage, and he can watch himself and correct errors in posture or in other ways improve his voice or delivery in the course of the interview.

Television is the glamour medium. When everything works well, it can be a lot of fun for everyone, including the publicist.

Microphone Tips   The National Association of Broadcasters lists these "microphone tips" to help in preparing for a broadcast interview.

1. Most announcers try to maintain a distance of six to eight inches from the microphone. Some persons lean back in their chairs or speak at great distances from the microphone, creating a "lack of presence" or an "off-mike" sound. Both elbows should be on the table in front of you.

2. Because "plosive" sounds, such as "p" and "b" often create a "pop" on the air, it is a good idea to talk at an angle to the microphone rather than directly into it.

3. Remember that the microphone is a very sensitive instrument. You need not shout into it. Use your voice only in a way that will best communicate your message.

4. Remove staples or paper clips after numbering your pages. Avoid shuffling of papers. Remove bracelets or other jewelry that may create extraneous noise and avoid handling the microphone.

5. When in the studio, consider every microphone "LIVE." Unless you are absolutely sure that the microphone is "off," remain silent; or at least, watch your language. Following a program, maintain your silence until "the mike is dead."

PUBLIC SERVICE ANNOUNCEMENTS

Several TV stations publish information about public-service announcements to assist nonprofit organizations. The booklet published by WNBC-TV in New York is one of the best and is extremely useful in the preparation of PSA's for TV. The guidelines also include tips about the shipping of films and other advice relevant to other types of publicity materials. Following are excerpts.

Film Information
1. Send a maximum of two copies of each individual film.
2. Each individual box or reel should be clearly labeled with the name of the organization and the title and length of the film. *DO NOT* place this information on the tape which secures the film to the reel.
3. Film should be secured to the reel with easily removable tape, and the box or envelope in which the film is mailed should be easily opened.
4. We use l6mm film in lengths of 10, 20, 30, and 60 seconds.

Video Tape Information
1. Send only one copy of each individual tape or multireel.
2. Each individual tape reel should be clearly labeled with the name of the organization and the title and length of the tape. The box in which the tape is sent must be labeled with the organization name and address and title and length of announcement(s).
3. *Always* include either a storyboard or script of the announcement.
4. We use two-inch, high band, color video tape in lengths of 10, 20, 30 and 60 seconds.

Slide/Copy Information
1. Send a maximum of two copies of each individual slide.
2. Slides should be labeled with the name of the organization and

should be numbered in order of appearance.

3. Send only two copies of each individual script (copy). Scripts should indicate the point of appearance of each slide.
4. Slides should be mounted for television, in metal or plastic mounts and with horizontal image.
5. We use two by two inch, 35mm slides with copy in lengths of 10 and 20 seconds.
6. The number of words required for slide/copy announcements is as follows:
   10 seconds—20 to 25 words. (Maximum of two slides.)
   20 seconds—40 to 45 words. (Maximum of four slides.)
7. Remember, each digit of a telephone number or address is counted as a word.
8. Brevity and clarity should be the rule in writing scripts. Avoid awkward language, write short sentences and make every word count.

Background Information

A cover letter should always accompany all announcements. The letter should be on organization letterhead, should include the organization address and telephone number, and should be dated.

When sending announcements for the first time, include in the package the following information:

1. A copy of your Internal Revenue Service Tax Exemption Certificate.
2. Background information on your organization and/or the program featured in your announcement. This would include information on the size of your organization, approximate number of people you service, type of service(s) offered, method of service or treatment (e.g., drug-free rehabilitation), to whom your services are offered (e.g., the elderly or the handicapped) and other information of this type.
3. A copy of your latest annual report.
4. A list of your board of directors or administrators.
5. If your announcement is fund raising, send information on your organization's funding sources and a copy of your latest financial. statement.

Tags

A tag is a short identification used to localize a national organization's announcement or give information not included on the film such as a telephone number or an address.

We can insert a tag *only* if the film was made to accommodate it. There must be a minimum of five seconds at the end of the film to insert tag information slide. The announcement must time out to exactly 10, 20, 30 or 60 seconds, including the tag information.

We encourage organizations to have all information included on the film itself in order to eliminate the need for a tag. The use of a tag will delay the airing of your announcement because of the extra steps that must be taken before the announcement can be programmed.

Special Events   We cannot air announcements promoting any kind of special event or community events of a limited duration such as one day or two weeks. Examples of such events would include telethons, walkathons, dinners, dances, conferences, shows, etc.

General Information   *When to send* . . . Materials should be sent in at least three weeks prior to when you want them to start airing.

How long used . . . Generally, announcements are used for a period of six to nine months unless you indicate a specific campaign period or unless they are seasonal announcements.

How they are used . . . When your announcements have been received and cleared, they are then transferred onto Video Cartridge and are aired as Video Cartridges. This is why we need so few copies of film, tape or slides. The materials are then stored for a period and then discarded. Unfortunately, because of the great volume of materials we receive, we cannot return materials sent in.

WNBC-TV operates on a computer system. Your announcements are placed on a list with several other announcements during different time periods. Your announcement then rotates with the others and is aired according to availabilities.

This system does not allow us to inform you of the days and times your announcement will air. We do, however, send out a quarterly statement indicating the number of times your announcement aired during the quarter and the commercial dollar value of the air time we donated to your organization.

Help us serve you better . . . Advise us of:

1. Any major changes or restructuring of your organization.
2. Any change in executive director/president or public relations officer.
3. Any change in address or telephone number.
4. Any person featured in your announcement running for political office during election years.
5. Any limitations on the length of time your announcement can be aired.
6. Any other changes that would affect the usage of your announcement.

Radio Scripts   Many of these suggestions are useful in writing radio scripts or news releases specifically for broadcasters. In general, news releases for radio and TV stations should be shorter than those for print—shorter in total length and also in length of each sentence. The simpler the sentence construction, the better. Avoid parenthetical phrases or other interruptions. On the other hand, overly short sentences can be too choppy. Here's an offbeat tip:

Avoid pronouns. Listeners may have trouble identifying the person, so repeat the name and/or title. For the same reason, avoid figures, long words, hard-to-pronounce words. The best test is for you to read it aloud before submission.

COLUMNS AND BUREAUS

Columnists   Syndicated and local columnists are a tremendously important category for publicists, even though some, such as Walter Winchell, Louella Parsons, Dorothy Kilgallen, Hedda Hopper and others who became as famous as the people they chronicled, are no longer with us.

Earl Wilson, whose column appears in the New York Post and more than 100 other newspapers, once stated:

"Some of my best friends are press agents. In fact, practically all of my best friends are press agents."

The alert publicist can place items with syndicated columnists, even if his interests are not in the entertainment field.

It is possible to obtain mentions of hotels, restaurants, galleries, books, real estate projects and a multitude of new products, by providing the type of anecdote or other item which is consistent with the style of the particular columnist. Sometimes, columnists such as Earl Wilson even use photos.

Exclusives   The major point with most columnists is to make sure that the item is not only consistent with their style, but is provided on an exclusive basis. Publicists who specialize in column items often find that a good way to work with columnists is to provide them with a "free item," that is an item about a celebrity who is not a client of the publicist, or other news tips, thus giving the columnist useful material. The columnist then is likely to react on a quid pro quo basis and use the publicist's commercial material, provided it is accurate, exclusive and entertaining.

Show business, television, entertainment and gossip columnists are merely the top of the iceberg among syndicated features. Hundreds of nationally syndicated columnists are listed in Working Press, Editor & Publisher's annual syndicate issue and other directories, in categories which include beauty, business, etiquette, family, fashion, politics, sports and numerous special interests. Columnists such as Sylvia Porter, Abby, Ann Landers and Jack Anderson are more widely read than any other writers.

Most publicists are aware of the importance of the columnists, but do not regularly think of them as publicity contacts. One reason for this is that most of the columnists do not work in the headquarters office of their syndicates, but instead have offices in branch offices of the syndicates (particularly in New York and Washington) or at their "home newspapers," and publicists often do not know where to contact them. This information is a valuable asset of a unique directory, Syndicated Columnists.

The syndicates claim that they forward mail to their columnists. Some do. Sometimes. A few years ago, an executive of the Register and Tribune stated, "Millions of dollars in public relations money is wasted by sending press releases to syndicates. We throw away bushel baskets of press releases every week." Obviously, the loss is not millions of dollars, but it generally is wasteful to send news releases to syndicates.

In addition to nationally syndicated columnists, many newspapers have local columnists who also require exclusives and special material.

Action Line A relatively new type of column is the "Action Line" reporter or other type of consumer news column. The writer of these columns can be serviced with booklets, fact kits and other reference materials.

Photo Syndicates Syndicate and local column placement is not confined to text material. The Associated Press and United Press International operate *photo* divisions which distribute, by mail and wire, to thousands of outlets. In addition, several syndicates, particularly NEA and King, distribute photo pages. News and feature photos often are accepted from public relations sources, providing the photos are exclusive. Several syndicate editors require negatives, rather than prints, in order to guarantee exclusivity and also to enable them to do their own editing. This is expecially relevant for color photos. Feature photo editors are much more concerned with picture quality than their counterparts on the news side. Captions must be brief and the picture must be "obvious" and good enough to stand alone.

Bureaus Major newspapers, magazines, radio and TV stations and networks, wire services and other media maintain *bureaus* in Washington, state capitals and major cities. A majority of publicists totally ignore this important outlet for major publicity. Perhaps the major reason for this omission is that many publicists are not aware of the availability of this data in several directories, notably News Bureaus in the U.S., but also, on a local basis, in Hudson's Washington News Media and Calforina Publicity Outlets.

The best way to keep up-to-date with any publication is to

read it. This can be misleading in the case of various trade publications which publish, usually on the contents or editorial pages, names and addresses of "offices." These offices often are advertising sales offices and are not news bureaus.

An important auxiliary in making maximum use of these books is a map of the United States. A newspaper which is located near a state border is likely to have one or more bureaus in the adjacent state. For example, a news release about an event in Indiana should be sent to the appropriate Indiana bureau of the nearby Louisville (Kentucky) Courier-Journal. Similarly, check a map and you'll see why the Florida Times Union in Jacksonville maintains bureaus in Georgia.

If nothing else, users of these directories will increase their familiarity with the U.S. geography! For example, Memphis is located in the southwestern corner of Tennessee and the Commercial Appeal maintains bureaus in the adjacent states of Arkansas and Mississippi, as well as in Tennessee.

A few newspapers, such as The New York Times, list the street addresses of their bureaus, usually on the editorial page. However, telephone numbers and names of bureau chiefs usually are not included. Several of the magazines, such as Time and Newsweek, list bureau personnel, but not addresses.

The Hartford Courant maintains an extensive bureau system in Connecticut. A publicist with a news release about a person or event in New Britain, Conn., for example, not only should send it to the New Britain Daily Herald, but also to the Hartford Courant.

Many major newspapers have state, suburban and national news editors. A news release sent to the city editor may be referred to the proper editor, but it usually is more efficient, and a saving in time, to send it to the local bureau. A few newspapers, such as the Los Angeles Herald-Examiner, maintain bureaus, but prefer that news releases and other communications be sent only to their main offices.

Absolute caution: Never send the same news release to more than one bureau of a publication. This results in considerable confusion with operations which have a large number of bureaus, such as The Associated Press and United Press International.

The Wall Street Journal and the Fairchild publications, for example, are national newspapers with a large number of local bureaus which cover their territories with considerable diligence. Publicists, therefore, are reminded to send news releases to the appropriate local bureau.

It is important to repeat that the mastheads of many business publications list several addresses which often are advertising and business offices. News releases sent to such offices generally are thrown away and rarely are forwarded to the proper editorial office.

A few large-circulation magazines, including McCall's and Ladies' Home Journal, issue regional sections with local-interest features. However, these sections are produced at the main offices.

Several major newspapers issue suburban or regional editions. These usually are produced under the auspices of a suburban or regional editor, at the main office. However, in the case of the Chicago Tribune, Los Angeles Times and a few other newspapers, there are separate suburban offices.

Bureau personnel are changed more frequently than departmental editors or other staff members, and, in many cases, it is proper and preferable to address news releases to Bureau Chief rather than an individual name.

NOTES

PUBLICITY MATERIALS

This section consists of news releases and other publicity materials, with each item followed by comments about style, distribution and other specific details.

Since these are actual items and not theoretical forms prepared to illustrate textbook points, a reader can question various items, rewrite them and produce improvements. Many news releases are imperfect compromises, often reflecting the bias of the client; restrictions by attorneys, accountants and others; time pressures, and various considerations.

Several types of news releases are reprinted complete and verbatim. These were distributed exactly as reproduced here. Printed release forms were not used. Some publicists prefer letterheads or other printed identification, while others maintain that this is unnecessary and conceivably detracts from the headline and content. A small number of public relations agencies use different release forms for each client, with fashion and other special accounts often having special colors and paper textures, as well as logos and other design elements.

Agencies and large public relations departments sometimes use another special form for circulation of drafts, with a line, box or space for signature of the person or persons granting approval and planned date of distribution. This form may also include the media categories slated to receive the release. In such cases, the approval pre-release form is useful for filing and also for internal circulation.

It's all a matter of opinion and preference and is part of the variety of the publicity business.

These news releases were printed on standard 8½ x 11 white bond paper and mailed in standard #10 business envelopes.

The source (name, address and phone) or contact (sometimes

more than one) appear single-spaced in the upper left corner. An alternate format, though used less frequently, puts the contact information in the upper right corner. In either case, the release date generally is typed on the right side. There is nothing sacrosanct about any of this. Consistency of style is most important and the key rule simply is common sense.

Slug Line For example, news releases sometimes contain information for the editor or broadcaster, particularly with regard to exclusivity, and it is logical that this information be highlighted. The usual procedure is to use all-capital letters, referred to as "all caps," or underline and to position this below the contact data. A release might include one or more of the following "slug lines."

Exclusive To You
Written Expressly For (name)
Exclusive To (name of publication and/or person)
Exclusive To You In (city, state, region, country)
Exclusive To You In Your Field
For: Back-To-School Section
For: Annual Business Review Issue
Christmas Feature
Exclusive To You Until (date)
Advance For Release (date and possibly the hour—may be typed on two lines for emphasis)
Exclusive To You In (media category, e.g., newspapers, real estate trade publications)
Attention: Business News Editor (or Women's Editor or City Editor or other types of editors; more than one may be listed)

This type of data is called the "slug line" because of the custom of typesetters to use a slug, a strip of nonprinting metal, as a marker.

Headline Some publicists prefer not to use all caps for anything except the headline. The body of the news release and also the headline is double-spaced, but even this rule has exceptions and variations based on a common-sense reading of the specific news release. For example, a secondary headline above (an awning head) the main headline or below (subhead) often is typed upper case-lower case, rather than all caps, and might be single-spaced. An awning headline could be typed flush left, rather than centered and might be underlined. It could be a lead-in to the main headline, a phrase, a quote, comment or other type of "tease" and, in such cases, might be elliptical and preceded or followed by asterisks or dots (generally three dots).

Short headlines are preferable, as they are more likely to be used. For example, a two-line headline of 16 characters each can be used intact as a two-line, one-column newspaper headline. Similarly, a 32-character (counting each space and letter as one each) single line is desirable. However, this rarely is possible, and attempts to conform to this rule often result in strained writing.

Similarly, the production of a second line of exactly the same count as the first is not obligatory.

Neatness counts, and a professional appearance is laudable but content is more important. Of course, when possible, try not to divide a compound verb between lines of a headline or to end the first line of a headline with a preposition or other dangling words, and certainly do not hyphenate or divide words between lines.

However, the philosophy of this book is permissive with regard to many rules, and headline writing calls for more emphasis on creativity and use of colorful action phrases, and less concern with character counts. As with news release writing, don't go overboard with similes, metaphors, alliteration, puns and other figures of speech. Obviously, financial news, personnel announcements and other straight or hard news must be handled with dignity and a manner different from some types of features.

Information about photos or other materials (e.g., annual report, booklet, other releases) might be referred to in the upper or right corners, or, more generally, flush left at the end of the release, below the end marks (# # # has replaced -30- as the most common form for indicating the end of the last page; the end of other pages generally is indicated by -more-, which is typed in the center of the last line).

Caption There is as much, or more, variation in style of photo captions as news releases. Most photos are 8 x 10, and some publicists use 8 x 10 caption paper, rather than 8½ x 11. There's really little difference, and the overhang provides added protection. Special caption paper can be used in which, among other conveniences, the sheet is perforated about six inches from the top.

The caption may be typed twice—double-spaced on the upper portion and single-spaced on the lower portion. The lower part is pasted on the back of the photo and thus serves as a permanent reference. The upper part is folded so that it faces the photo and is below the photo when opened. The perforation merely aids in tearing off the upper part so that it can be sent to the typesetter. In some cases, it is helpful to number the photo print and caption and to refer to this number in the cover letter or at the end of the release.

Financial NOTE: This book does not discuss specialized types of news releases which require special formats and distribution. For example, financial releases, particularly those reporting on sales, earnings, dividends and other details about the business of publicly owned companies, generally are accompanied by tables comparing various data for the current and preceding fiscal years. These charts generally are appended on a separate sheet. This type of publicity material must be carefully checked and approved by accountants, attorneys and others, but the final responsibility for everything, including proofreading, is that of the publicist. This sometimes is difficult because of the many people involved and the pressure for "immediate disclosure."

Asterisks and footnotes often are necessary in order to provide further explanation with regard to the tabular matter. All of this is part of the expertise of the financial publicist *and* the typist.

Another type of specialized release deals with books, in which vital data is summarized (sometimes single-spaced) at the beginning or end of the release. This data should include title, author, publisher, number of pages, retail price, type of binding (hard or paper) and publication date. The timing of distribution varies; ideally, galley proofs or unbound copies should be sent to the book trade press several months prior to the publication date. Bound copies should be sent to other reviewers two months prior to publication date or as far in advance as possible.

Show business releases follow a similar pattern, particularly with regard to a listing of "credits," i.e., cast and other personnel.

Food releases often are accompanied by recipes which are typed in a special format, with the ingredients sometimes single-spaced and the text double-spaced. This is done merely to save space, and all releases should be double-spaced whenever possible.

The following pages photographically reproduce news releases to show typical formats or are typeset to conserve space. The sections in italics indicate the author's comments about the preceding releases.

From: Richard Weiner, Inc.
       888 Seventh Ave., N.Y. 10019
       (212) 582-7373

For: Sandoz Pharmaceuticals

For Immediate Release

SEXUALITY AND THE AGING IS SUBJECT OF NEW SURVEY OF PHYSICIANS

Disparity in sexual desire between older spouses and sex-related complaints of elderly widows and widowers are two of the major issues emerging from a new survey on sexuality and the aging conducted among physicians throughout the country who specialize in treating older patients.

The survey by Sandoz Pharmaceuticals, East Hanover, N.J., revealed that 47% of elderly husbands and 36% of wives expressed the desire for more frequent sexual relations. Unequal sexual interest is believed by a majority (53%) of physicians responding to be a source of conflict in at least a quarter of older marriages.

The survey shows that sexual problems are common in the elderly widowed. Thirty-four percent of physicians responding said that their widowed patients frequently express specific sexual problems or show vague or psychosomatic complaints strongly suggestive of sexual desire. Such problems are reported occasionally by the widowed men and women to 49 percent of physicians responding.

The main reasons cited by physicians for sexual inactivity among the aged are lack of suitable partner (35%), loss of ability to perform (30%), and lack of interest (23%).

- more -

99

Among the conditions reported by physicians as most often associated with sexual incapacity in the aged are, in descending order of frequency: vascular (65%), genitourinary (64%), psychiatric (56%), drug-related (50%), endocrinologic (47%), cardiac (42%), neurologic (28%), and liver (9%).

A majority of physicians asserted that postmenopausal vaginitis is responsible for sexual dysfunction in less than a third of all postmenopausal patients.

According to the survey, single hormone therapy for sexual dysfunction is often used for both sexes, while combined therapy is more common for females. When hormone therapy is elected, 70 percent of physicians employ a single hormone for males, androgen, while physicians are about equally divided on the use for females of either estrogen alone or estrogen/androgen.

On the controversial subject of whether physicians should initiate inquiries about sexual function among their elderly patients, a large majority (87%) agreed with the statement: "Giving patients an opportunity to ventilate their sexual preoccupation may prove the way to renewed sexual expression, adding a positive element to their lives and serving to allay the varying degrees of depression characteristic of this period."

The survey was conducted by Sandoz Pharmaceuticals as part of its continuing Enquiry Into Aging project. This service enables physicians to compare their approach to caring for elderly patients with the collective experience of colleagues throughout the country. The survey incorporated the responses of 1500 physicians nationally.

From: Richard Weiner, Inc.
        888 Seventh Ave., N.Y. 10019
        (212) 582-7373

For: The Saturday Review, Carll Tucker (246-9700)

For Release: March 8, 1977

THE SATURDAY REVIEW ACQUIRED BY GROUP HEADED BY CARLL TUCKER

- - -

Norman Cousins to Remain Editor

The Saturday Review has been acquired by a group headed by Carll Tucker, 25, who will be the magazine's new president. The announcement was made this afternoon (Tuesday) in New York by Norman Cousins, longtime editor of the magazine; Carll Tucker, and R. Peter Straus, president of radio station WMCA.

Norman Cousins will continue as editor and R. Peter Straus will be chairman of the executive committee of the new company, Saturday Review Magazine Corp. Mr. Tucker informed the staff this morning that no major personnel or format changes are contemplated.

Mr. Cousins, who was 25 years old when the magazine was placed in his hands by its founders, Henry Seidel Canby and Amy Loveman, said he was gratified by the "symmetry" of this arrangement. "I feel fortunate and grateful to have found investors and a successor, Carll Tucker, who will carry on The Saturday Review's tradition of independence and integrity," said Mr. Cousins.

- more -

101

Mr. Tucker, who will be deeply involved in both the editorial and the business sides of the magazine, described The Saturday Review as "intellectually ambitious, calm and reasonable at a time when even intelligent magazines strain to outshriek each other on the newsstands. Above all, The Saturday Review is independent of the megacorporations which are munching magazines like crackers.

"With Norman Cousins' help, I intend to make The Saturday Review continue to grow in interest, scope, involvement, seriousness and liveliness. Above all, I want to get Saturday Review into the hands of every reader who might enjoy it. Now more than ever, we need an independent, intelligent voice to prevent us from being swept up in the hysteria and faddishness of our popular press," said Mr. Tucker.

A fifth-generation journalist, Carll Tucker was a theater and book critic for the Village Voice and a free-lance writer whose work has appeared in The New York Times, The New York Times Magazine and The New Republic. He is a 1973 graduate of Yale (summa cum laude, Phi Beta Kappa). Mr. Tucker's parents founded and published the Patent Trader newspaper in Mt. Kisco, N.Y. His wife, Diane Straus Tucker, is executive editor of the Cranford Citizen and Chronicle, in Cranford, New Jersey.

Mr. Tucker pointed out that The Saturday Review has one of the best-educated readerships in the country (60 percent college graduates), the highest median income of any group of subscribers except those of the business magazines, the highest percentage of professionals (40 percent), and, as of this year, the largest gain in young adult readers.

- more -

Founded in 1924 and originally called The Saturday Review of Literature, The Saturday Review is currently a biweekly which includes reviews in all the arts, as well as special sections devoted to science, travel, environment, communications and other subjects of vital interest to well-educated adults. The Saturday Review has an unusually loyal readership, with 60 percent committed to long-term subscriptions and more than two-thirds who subscribe at full rates.

The Saturday Review's distinguished staff of editors and regular contributors includes Goodman Ace, Cleveland Amory, James Cass, John Ciardi, Jacques-Yves Cousteau, Judith Crist, R. Buckminster Fuller, Roland Gelatt, Irving Kolodin, Katharine Kuh, Albert Rosenfeld, Leo Rosten, Horace Sutton, Walter Terry and Peter Young. Mr. Cousins has presided over the staff as editor-in-chief for 35 years. The company moved last week to new offices at 1290 Avenue of the Americas.

Mr. Cousins took over the editorship of The Saturday Review in 1940, when its circulation was 20,000. "There was something of an unwritten law that no magazine of ideas could have a circulation of more than 30,000," said Mr. Cousins. "I think that was a lot like the four-minute mile, and when we cracked through the barrier we really took off." Today, the magazine's circulation is more than half a million, which is greater than all of the "quality" magazines, including, for example, The New Yorker.

From: Steve Schwartz
      Richard Weiner, Inc.
      888 Seventh Ave., N.Y. 10019
      (212) 582-7373

For: Mature Temps, Inc.

For Release: June 1, 1977

EMPLOYMENT SERVICE REPORTS ABUNDANCE OF TEMPORARY JOBS

FOR COLLEGE STUDENTS THIS SUMMER

With college expenses soaring, students and their parents
will be happy to learn that temporary jobs for college students
will be plentiful this summer. Such jobs will enable students
who work the entire summer to earn a substantial amount towards
their college expenses.

"Because we have more jobs available nationally than we can
fill, we feel that college students home on vacation will become
a major resource for us to turn to," reports Richard Ross, president
of Mature Temps, a nationwide temporary employment service. Most
of the positions available to them will be office jobs requiring
skills such as typing and other secretarial skills or proofreading.

According to current tax laws, a full-time student may earn
an unlimited amount of money without negating the family's tax
deduction, provided that the family contributes more than one-half
toward the student's total support.

Mature Temps, which specializes in placing workers with mature
work attitudes, has offices in New York City; White Plains (N.Y.);
Philadelphia; Plymouth Meeting (Pa.); Bala Cynwyd (Pa.); Los Angeles;
Pasadena; Baltimore; Washington, D.C.; Boston; Chicago, Houston;
Dallas, and San Francisco.

# # #

104

These three news releases have been reproduced in a smaller page size than the 8½ x 11 plain white sheets of paper on which they were originally printed.

The first release, on sexuality and the aging, was utilized by several news magazines and other national media. It's a newsworthy subject, and the release is crammed with data, without being too technical. The first sentence is much too long, though it's comprehensible.

The use of parentheses generally should be avoided, but the insertion of statistics within parentheses works well here because reporters thus can see the data easily and then delete the parenthetical material, if they wish.

The client, Sandoz Pharmaceuticals, was mentioned only twice, in the second paragraph and in the last paragraph. A third mention could have been included without getting too commercial. For example, the third paragraph on page two could have started with, "According to the Sandoz survey . . ."

The second release was more timely and was announced at a news conference. The client was The Saturday Review, and the phone number of the magazine's new owner was included, in addition to the phone number of the p.r. agency.

The three-page news release is a combination of news about the sale of The Saturday Review by Norman Cousins with background facts about the new owner and the magazine itself. Interwoven are quotations from the principals, which is an opportunity to promote the publications and the individuals. The quotations combine conventional plaudits with a few pithy, colorful remarks.

The youthfulness of the new publisher, Carll Tucker, was newsworthy, and his age, therefore, was indicated in the first sentence.

The release was accompanied by photos of Messrs. Cousins and Tucker, and the photo captions featured additional biographical data (the titles of Mr. Cousins' books, awards and honors).

The third release is less newsworthy or consequential and, in fact, is quite "commercial." It was used by the media because it was brief, timely and offered a "consumer benefit." The last paragraph listed all of the local offices of the company. Another version of this release, with a local address fill-in, was distributed to newspapers in the branch office cities.

In each of these releases, the headline capsulizes the story. The headlines are long, though not cumbersome. Abbreviations, contractions, numerals and phrases, rather than complete sentences, may be used in a headline, as the major purpose is to summarize the news release and not necessarily to write the headline which will appear with the published article.

Styles vary, and consistency within a release is more important than rigid adherence to The New York Times, The Associated

Press or other standards of journalistic style. For example, in this release, numbers under 10 are spelled out. There are occasions when numerals are used for numbers under 10, such as when they appear in a series or as part of a sentence with many numerals, including those over 10. Numerals generally are used for all ages, such as 7-year-old, rather than seven-year-old.

Brevity, unity, coherence still are vital, and publicists tend to write long-winded, cluttered sentences in an attempt to cram in lots of information. Often the motivation is to bury the plug so it is innocuous.

In general, it is not helpful to set arbitrary lengths or other restrictions. However, after a release is written, the writer or another person should reread it. Sometimes, reading it aloud helps in editing and also shows up incorrect or loose grammar, difficult words, repetitions, awkward phrases, run-on sentences, incoherent construction, unclear antecedents and other weaknesses. A well-written release often has a flow, a rhythm and a style which is a joy to the publicist, the client and the media. Everyone benefits from good writing.

The use of unattributed opinions should be avoided in all forms of journalism. Publicity writing generally follows the same rules and guidelines used by journalists, except that the bias of the publicity source is reflected in the choice of subject matter and the reference to the source (the "client"). However, pejorative or "loaded words," excessive adjectives, superlatives and non-objective writing should be avoided and publicists should strive to maintain higher-than-average standards of journalism.

From: PR agency's name, address and phone

For: Lesney Products Corporation

For Immediate Release, Feb. 12

CAPT. PEG LEG AND HOOK INTRODUCED BY LESNEY

Pirates will be big with boys this year.

Lesney Products Corporation today introduced Fighting Furies, a new line of action figures featuring two pirates, Captain Peg Leg and his mate, Hook.

Male action-adventure figures are a $100-million market, and Elliott Harrowe, president of Lesney, predicts a sizable increase due to Peg Leg and Hook.

The 8½-inch figures, which will retail for about $5 each, are outfitted in authentically detailed pirate garb and are fully articulated with Action-Flex bodies. Additional arm movement, including dueling, is produced by pressing a button at the waist of the vinyl figure.

Action settings, complete with disguises, gear and comic book, retail for $5 to $7 and enable users to create imaginative adventures. The settings include the Captain Blood Adventure, Spanish Main Adventure, One-Eye Sailor Adventure, Hooded Falcon Adventure, Red Coat Adventure and Kung Fu Adventure. A play environment area, which opens into the deck of a Spanish galleon with helm bridge, anchor, rope and other props, retails for about $12 and also serves as a storage-carrying case.

Lesney, makers of the Matchbox cars, will launch Fighting Furies with the biggest advertising campaign in the company's history. The commercials feature Mason Reese, the 7-year-old television personality who has signed an exclusive contract with Lesney in the toy and hobby field. Lesney's primary market is boys.

"Most TV commercials for toys and other children's items feature loud music, a high-pressure announcer and angle shots to enlarge the product," states Harold Levine, president of Levine, Huntley, Schmidt, advertising agency for Lesney. "The Lesney Fighting Furies commercials," notes Mr. Levine, "consist solely of Mason Reese demonstrating the actual-size products and straightforwardly talking to other children."

The three 30-second spots, which already have been approved by the National Association of Broadcasters, will be shown to buyers at next week's Toy Fair exactly as they will be broadcast in the fall. This is uncommon in the toy industry, states Mr. Levine, "since nonapproved commercials often are previewed in extended versions in order to bedazzle buyers."

"The pirate concept and our treatment of it are likely to produce a tremendous impact," predicts Mr. Harrowe. "Our research with families indicates that pirates are anti-establishment and yet acceptable because of their independence, bravery and romantic role as free-lance, swashbuckling roamers of the seas.

"The lure of the high seas has always held a special place in the imaginations of boys of all ages. We feel that our Fighting Furies will create the right atmosphere for boys to play out their adventure fantasies," states Mr. Harrowe.

# # #

Submitted on PR agency's letterhead

News Conference About Pirates

You are cordially invited to meet:
Captain Peg Leg, 8½ inches, brand new

Hook, 8½ inches, brand new

Mason Reese, 44 inches, 7 years old

A news conference will be held 10:30 a.m., Tuesday, February 12, by Lesney Products Corporation (makers of Matchbox cars) in Room 534 of 200 Fifth Avenue (23rd Street) to introduce Fighting Furies, a new line of pirate figures.

Male action figures are a $100-million market and Elliot Harrowe, president of Lesney, predicts that the romantic adventure appeal of the Lesney dueling pirates will capture children's imaginations and the Toy Fair.

Mason Reese, who has an exclusive contract with Lesney in the toy and hobby field, will discuss Fighting Furies, and Harold Levine, president of the Levine, Huntley, Schmidt advertising agency, will show television commercials featuring Mason Reese. The biggest ad campaign in Lesney's history is a low-key, child-to-child approach, which is unusual in the toy industry.

The pirates are coming, on Tuesday morning, February 12.

# # #

From: PR agency's name, address and phone

For: Lesney Products Corporation

For Immediate Release, Feb. 12

THINK PIRATE

Captain Peg Leg and his first mate, Hook, are two pirates who will become better known this year.

The action figures, together with adventure settings, were unveiled today by Lesney Products Corporation, Moonachie, N.J. Elliott Harrowe, president of Lesney, predicts that the Fighting Furies—Peg Leg and Hook—will stimulate a tremendous interest in real and fictional pirates of the past.

How many of these pirates do you recall:

Capt. John Avery, Blackbeard, Francis Drake, Capt. Flint, John Hawkins, Capt. William Kidd, Sir John Killigrew, Jean LaFitte, Peter Legrand, Sir Henry Mainwaring, Sir Henry Morgan, Bartholomew Sharp, Sir Francis Verney, Capt. John Warde.

The concept of pirates generally conjures up images of stolen treasure—caskets of buried jewels, chests of gold dubloons and pieces of eight buried along the shores of unexplored sea coasts. This image has been supported over the years by fiction writers who have portrayed many pirates as good guys who have taken away ill-gotten treasure from evil forces. By today's standards, pirates would be considered members of a counterculture. They bucked the establishment by taking whatever they wanted and seemingly made up their own rules as they went along. Although each captain set the specific rules aboard his ship, there were certain traditions that everyone sailing under the Jolly Roger had to observe. The captain was given authority by his crew and could be disposed of by majority vote. As captain, he was entitled to his own cabin and a double share of all booty. Anyone, including the captain, caught cheating the rest of the crew would be punished. A captain's authority could be challenged at any time; therefore, the captain always felt the need to remind his crew that he was the strongest hand aboard the vessel. He would have to fight harder, drink harder and swear harder than any man aboard.

Among the most successful pirates were those who fought under the title of buccaneers or privateers. They attacked merchant ships, but only those supposedly belonging to the enemies of the country that commissioned them. Such men as Edward Morgan, William Kidd and Francis Drake were pirates and also patriots, splitting their booty with the crown that issued their commission. Privateering is one of the reasons that England became "Mistress of the Sea."

The most famous and flamboyant pirate probably was Edward Teach, also known as "Bluebeard," but the greatest of all pirates probably was Bartholomew Roberts, who is credited with the capture of over 400 ships. (He also supposedly awarded additional monies from captured prizes to members of the crew who lost limbs during the battle. Some historians say that this was the forerunner to our present policy of workmen's compensation.)

The most famous pirate story ever written is Robert Louis Stevenson's "Treasure Island," which was based on the exploits of real-life pirates. "Treasure Island," as told through the eyes of Jim Hawkins, gave its readers an insight into pirate traditions and lore and helped create the stereotype of the peg-leg pirate.

The glamorization of the pirate role took a giant step in the 1930's when Hollywood began to produce the "Swashbuckler," starring such perennial pirates as Douglas Fairbanks (Sr. and Jr.) and Errol Flynn.

Indeed, the Lesney pirates may stimulate the nostalgia and fantasy lives of many adults, as well as children. Certainly, Captain Peg Leg and Hook will help in geography lessons. Among the global pirates were the Barbary corsairs, the Moorish pirates and those who hovered near the coasts of Algeria, Tunis, Genoa and Tripoli.

Finally, there were the women pirates—Anne Bonney, China Ching, Han Cho and Mary Read were among the most successful.

But our lesson on pirates can end on the lighter side. Think, for example, of Gilbert and Sullivan's "Pirates of Penzance," and Cyril Ritchard. That's O.K. with Lesney, as long as you think pirate.   **109**

Product News Release

The news from Lesney Products is in the second paragraph. The first paragraph is a short sentence designed to capture reader interest. Thus, a "straight" news release is given a feature "twist."

The third paragraph presents a quote and a business angle, so the same release provides the multitude of details of interest to various types of trade and business media, but weaving in quotes or other feature material.

Prices and other dollar figures generally are typed as numerals and not spelled out, including figures below 10. In giving dollar figures which do not include cents, it is not necessary to indicate the cents, e.g., five dollars should be typed as $5 and not $5. or $5.00. The two zeros are redundant and can result in a typographical error or misinterpretation or misreading as five hundred dollars. Sometimes a figure is written out, and the numerals are inserted in following parentheses. Fractions generally are not spelled out, even when under 10.

The present tense is used in attributing the quotes in this release, i.e., predicts, states, says. It is equally appropriate to use the past tense.

Journalists perennially try to use alternate words for "he said." There are other words, but beware of stumbling for the sake of variety. For example, it generally is prudent to avoid words as declared, exclaimed, explained, as they may be pejorative.

In some cases, however, action verbs and colorful writing are called for. Similarly, it is permissible to end sentences with prepositions, as in the preceding sentence. News release writing need not be bland and should not be dull.

The release was distributed at a news conference held in the company's showroom. The invitation *to the news conference was written in the same low-key vein, a combination of "hard news" with color and a bit of humor. The invitation was printed on letterhead paper. The site of the conference was the company's showroom—commercial, but logical.*

A background feature *accompanied the news release in a press kit. The background feature was an attempt to add colorful historical material which might stimulate a magazine or newspaper supplement article, syndicated column or even an incidental reference by a broadcaster. The kit also included two captioned photos.*

From: PR agency's name, address and phone.

For: Muscular Dystrophy Associations of America, Inc.

TIME: Sunday, March 10, at 1 p.m.

PLACE: Van Cortlandt Mansion, Broadway and West 246 Street, The Bronx

EVENT: Hundreds to walk 15 miles to raise funds for the fight
against muscular dystrophy

Bronx people of all ages will participate in the Jerry Lewis
Walk-A-Thon Sunday, March 10, to raise funds for the fight
against muscular dystrophy. Walkers in the 15-mile event are
sponsored by local merchants and friends who pledge a specific
amount for each mile walked. All proceeds go to Muscular
Dystrophy Association of America, Inc.

Among dignitairies planning to attend are Bronx Borough
President Robert Abrams, NYC Comptroller Harrison J.
Goldin, State Senator Abraham Bernstein, Assemblymen
Anthony J. Mercorella, Burton G. Hecht and Oliver G. Koppell
and Councilman Stanley Simon.

The new Bronx MDAA poster child, 10-year-old Carlos
Mareno, will also be present.

YOUR COVERAGE IS INVITED

# # #

From: PR agency's name, address and phone

Plans for the United Nations University will be discussed by
Harold Taylor (former president of Sarah Lawrence University),
Buckminster Fuller, Glenn Olds (president of Kent State
University) and other founding members of the U.S. Committee
for the United Nations University at a news conference Tuesday
afternoon, November 20, at 2:30 p.m., at the Carnegie
Endowment International Center, U.N. Plaza at 46 Street, New
York.

Details of a $100-million grant from a government to establish
a campus will be announced.

# # #

*The following invitation was submitted in letter form on client's
stationery:*

October 19

Dear Editor:
You are cordially invited to join Freehold Mayor Romeo
Cascaes and other civic officials at the groundbreaking of
Wemrock Farm.

The event will be held Saturday morning, October 27, at 11:30
a.m., at Wemrock Farm, a 1400-unit residential community to be
built on a 180-acre site near Freehold. The entrance is on
Wemrock Road, off of Route 537, near the Greater Freehold
Area Hospital. **111**

Following the brief ceremonies at the site, we will have lunch at the American Hotel on Main Street in Freehold. We promise good food and no speeches.

We sincerely believe that Wemrock will be a major contribution to the growth of this area and hope that you will be able to join us. Would you please call my office, indicating your acceptance.

Cordially,
Gene A. Genola

Tip Sheets   *The Muscular Dystrophy event was announced with a tip sheet sent to news assignment directors of radio and TV stations, photo assignment editors of newspapers and wire services, and news editors.*

A common format is to list the Who, What, Where and When. In this case, the sheet starts with Time, Place and Description of Event, and then follows with the details.

The time (Sunday afternoon) was not ideal for news coverage, and the event was not unique. But it was covered! And the tip sheet also served to provide caption identifications for the newspaper photographers.

Daily newspapers, radio and TV stations prepare their assignments on the same day and the preceding day of events. In this case, the invitation was mailed to local media on Thursday morning, so that it almost certainly was received on Friday, rather than the day before the event, which was a Saturday. Because of the vagaries of mail delivery, it is prudent to mail this type of news tip sheet two days prior to the event, even when the event is scheduled for a weekday. Other types of invitations, such as news conferences, fashions, luncheons and events of interest to feature writers and specialized reporters (instead of, or in addition to, the city desks and news departments), often are mailed more than a day or two prior to the event.

The United Nations University event was announced in a slightly different format. It was brief, but included a great deal of information written as a news release in anticipation of publicity prior to the event. It was written in the style of the wire service "day books" and was used in their schedules of forthcoming news events. The news highlights were underlined to flag the attention of busy recipients.

Part of the news was revealed in the tip sheet, for example, $100-million grant, but the identity of the government (Japan) was not released until the event.

Another format is a letter of invitation, which was used by Wemrock Associates for local media. A pre-release accompanied the letter, a particularly useful service for weeklies and a good technique in this case because the event had to be scheduled on a Saturday.

From: PR Agency's name, address and phone

For: Lexington School for the Deaf

For Immediate Release, Jan. 9

LIPREADING CLASS FOR ADULTS TO BE HELD IN QUEENS

A lipreading course for hearing-handicapped adults will be conducted at the Lexington Hearing and Speech Center in Queens, starting January 22.

The 10 sessions, to be held on Tuesday afternoons from 1 to 2:30 p.m., will provide lipreading instruction, hearing aid evaluation and other tutoring and counseling. The class will meet at the Lexington School for the Deaf, 30th Avenue and 75th Street, Jackson Heights. The total fee is $35.

Information can be obtained from Dr. Martha Rubin, director of the center, at (212) 899-8800.

* * *

Brief News Release   *News releases should not be padded. The Lexington School release had only 11 lines and was for local media. A few used it verbatim, including the phone number.*

From: PR agency's name, address and phone
                                     HAPPY NEW YEAR
For: Lexington School for the Deaf

For Immediate Release, Jan. 2

TEACHERS FROM NEPAL, GREECE AND LATIN AMERICA LIVE AT LEXINGTON SCHOOL FOR THE DEAF IN QUEENS

Indira Shrestha is the founder and principal of the only school for deaf children in the country of Nepal. Located in the Himalayan Mountains in the capitol city, Kathmandu, the school currently is operating without its principal because Mrs. Shrestha is on a leave of absence. She is working as a teacher-aide in the preschool department of the Lexington School for the Deaf in Queens, N.Y., and hopes to start a program for hearing-impaired infants, and also a teacher-training program for deaf education, when she returns to Nepal.

Mrs. Shrestha lives, with her husband, at the Lexington School campus in Jackson Heights. The training of teachers from all over the United States and many other countries always has been an important function at the Lexington School and this year there are seven foreign student teachers at the school.

Venetta Lampropoulos, from Athens, Greece, is here with her husband. The foreign student teachers also include Mrs. Angela Nani of Buenos Aires, Argentina; Mrs. Nelssy Campos of Bogota, Colombia; Miss Behnaz Nesvaderani of Tehran, Iran, and Miss Amalia Camacho and Francisco Cordero of Costa Rica.

The six women and one man all work at the Lexington School for the full academic year and most of them also are enrolled at Columbia University or Queens College in order to study English or obtain advanced degrees.

The Lexington program provides specialized, practical training in oral communication to speak and read lips, and the natural language approach of teaching deaf children. The Lexington service courses emphasize infant and preschool training; audiology, with stress on the diagnosis, evaluation, and rehabilitation of hearing problems; multimedia teaching aids; the integration of deaf children into hearing schools, and other programs which are unique at the Lexington School.

The schedule for each student teacher is different, according to their background and interests. Mrs. Shrestha is unusual because of her extensive experience. In 1969, she received a master's degree from Smith College in Massachusetts where she majored in education of the deaf. After a brief period at the Lexington School, she returned to her native Nepal where she started the country's first school for the deaf.

The two Costa Ricans, Francisco Cordero and Amalia Camacho, also previously studied at Lexington. Last year, Mr. Cordero worked in a hearing aid testing program. He currently is studying speech and audiology at Queens College and teaching Spanish to high school students at Lexington. Miss Camacho, who has taught hearing children in Costa Rica, is interested in speech and auditory training.

The two South Americans also have had specialized teaching experience. Mrs. Campos taught multiply-handicapped children, including aphasia and mental retardation. Mrs. Nani taught deaf children in Argentina for several years before coming to New York in 1972.

Miss Nesvaderani, who has a degree in social work, taught deaf children in Iran. Mrs. Lampropoulos, who received her college degree in home economics, has taught deaf children in Athens for three years.

The foreign student teachers at the Lexington School often are sponsored by parent-teacher associations or civic organizations in the United States or their native countries.

Photo is of Indira Shrestha of Nepal. Other photos available from Ken Tremaine at Lexington School, 899-8800.

* * *

From: PR agency's name, address and phone

For: The Ridge Tool Company

For Release at Will

NEW CROP OF CALENDARS ON THE WAY; ONE COMPANY PRINTS 600,000 COPIES

With the approach of another year, a new crop of calendars is on the way, destined for hanging in such diverse places as plumbing shops, factories, kitchens and dormitories all over America. Though fashions change, pinups remain an enduring favorite for the new year's guide to what day of the month it is.

Pinups have been used to decorate U.S. calendars since early in the century and have proved an irresistible attraction to generations of girl watchers. Subjects were reproduced from paintings, drawings and photos. Among the best-known have been "September Morn," the Petty girls and Marilyn Monroe.

Yet, the staple of pinup calendars has always been little-known but generously endowed beauties. One of those, who has moved up to film stardom, was Raquel Welch, seen in a bikini in 1965 on a calendar published by the Ridge Tool Company of Elyria, Ohio.

Peter Gowland, the nation's foremost photographer of girls, took the Raquel Welsh picture and scores of others during the more than 10 years he has been lensing American beauties for the Ridge calendars, which have reached a printing of 600,000 with the current issue.

One of the first pinups to illustrate a calendar was "Colette," a portrait painting of an attractive young woman by Angelo Asti, printed in 1903 by Brown & Bigelow, the St. Paul, Minnesota, calendar company and advertising specialty manufacturer. The idea must have caught the public fancy, because the same manufacturer put out a more enticing portrait of a long-haired beauty by another artist the following year under the title of "Meditation."

Pinup calendars were being printed by other specialty houses as the decade ended. It was not until 1913, however, that nude art appeared as a decorative incentive to tell the day of the month with the publication of the "September Morn" calendar from the French oil, "Matinee Septembre," by Paul Chabas. The painting, which had become the subject of a censorship controversy, was printed by calendar firms in millions of copies.

A pioneer artist of the nearly clad and unclothed feminine figure in calendar art was Rolf Armstrong, whose work in the 1920's set a style for the future. Others included George Petty and Varga. Petty's work also adorned a calendar issued in 1952 by The Ridge Tool Company. This type of art became so popular in the 1940's that *Esquire* published its Varga calendars for a nicely turned profit.

Then came the Marilyn Monroe nude, erupting a new constellation in the calendar firmament. Photographed by Tom Kelley, it was used in a 1951 calendar—and sales soared to the millions. The photo had been taken when Marilyn was an unknown and needed the $50 modeling fee. The photo came to light as she began to emerge in films, but she capitalized on the notoriety by publicizing it instead of disputing it. Screen actresses Jayne Mansfield and Diana Dors, on the other hand, sought public notice by being photographed, if in less revealing fashion, for pinup calendars.

Pinup photos for calendars can be tasteful as well as decorative, in the opinion of glamour photographer Peter Gowland. His pictures adorn the most widely distributed, commercially sponsored pinup calendar, the one issued by The Ridge Tool Company. Though 600,000 copies have been printed for the latest edition, only the industrial, electrical, plumbing, hardware and other users of Ridge tools receive it. So, now you know what your plumber's been looking at.

* * *

Feature News Release

There's no "hard news" in these articles; the first is about the foreign teachers who live for a year or more at a school in New York. The training program is not new, and this year's group started several months ago.

Let's face the problem. Most publicists rarely, if ever, have the opportunity to prepare news releases about monumentally important news. How do you publicize a project which is worthwhile but not hot news? How do you make it newsworthy without exaggerating? Here's one solution—a feature news release.

Note the timing. It was distributed during the last week in December, one of the slowest news weeks—an opportune time for publicists. The release was dated several days ahead to allow the recipients time to rewrite, interview, photograph or react in other ways. The writer added a Happy New Year above the January 2 release date, which surely did not detract from the release and provided a special touch.

The release was accompanied by one captioned photo, and the end of the release included a note about the availability of other photos.

In addition to local media, the mailing went to foreign correspondents in New York representing media in Nepal, Greece and the other countries mentioned in the release. In each case, the specific country was circled in the release.

Another example of a feature news release is the article about calendars. It was undated, hence the phrase, For Release at Will.

116

Sent to Sunday supplement editors and other users of features, it was accompanied by one or more photos, depending on the publication.

The name of the company—the "plug"—does not appear until the end of the third paragraph—but still it's on page one. The company name is mentioned twice on each of the next two pages, but in a way which is relevant. The article, though written for the general reader, includes a good amount of factual material and thus could be rewritten or condensed by various types of editors and broadcasters.

From: PR agency's name, address and phone

For: The Ridge Tool Company

Suggested Editorial

Nothing goes swifter than the years, the Roman poet Ovid observed. And the unrelenting passage of time is brought to mind with the approach of another year.

Past memories and visions of the future, yes, even the snows of yesteryear, are evoked by the appearance of a new calendar. A neat tabular arrangement of the days of each month and week, it is humankind's habitual way of reckoning the chronology of everyday living.

And what is a calendar without adornment? Landscapes, Currier and Ives prints, animals, babies and comic figures are typical illustrations. The form divine has been used to decorate U.S. calendars since early in the century and has proved an irresistible pinup attraction to generations of girl watchers.

Feminine pulchritude has been reproduced from paintings, drawings and photos. Well-known subjects have included "September Morn," the Petty girls and an unadorned Marilyn Monroe.

So, here it is December. The new calendars are beginning to come in—$150 million worth nationally—from banks, insurance companies, airlines and even neighborhood enterprises. One manufacturing concern, The Ridge Tool Company of Elyria, Ohio, prints 600,000 copies, lavishly illustrated in color with pinup photos, for free distribution to its customers throughout the world. A model of propriety, the Ridge calendar pinups reveal no more than can be seen at the average beach or pool.

Devotees of calendar art will soon be hanging their trophies in such diverse places as plumbing shops, factories, kitchens and dormitories all over America. Though fashions change, pinups remain an enduring favorite for a comelier look at the year to come.

* * *

117

Editorial subjects are as varied as news articles and range from serious controversial issues to light human-interest features. Here's one of the latter. The "suggested editorial," about a commercial calendar, was accompanied by a brief letter, individually addressed to the editorial-page editor, and a sample of the calendar.

From: PR agency's name, address and phone

For: The Ridge Tool Company

70 MILLION WRENCHES

You don't have to be a plumber or professional craftsman to know the difference between a Stillson and a monkey wrench, between a single-headed and a double-headed end wrench. Among the many types of pipe wrenches, the two best known are the Stillson and the Ridgid.

The Stillson wrench, invented by Daniel Stillson, an American, in 1869, has a jaw which tightens as pressure is applied to the handle and is used primarily for turning pipes.

The Ridgid pipe wrench also is an American development, and 1978 is its 55th anniversary.

Jack Dempsey was heavyweight champion of the world, the Charlston was the big dance craze, *Time* magazine was founded, "Abie's Irish Rose" was an established Broadway hit, and Bobby Jones had won the first of what were to be his four National Open golf championships.

The time was 1923. A handful of employees of The Ridge Tool Company, which had just been formed in Ridgeville, Ohio, was beginning to manufacture the company's first product, the heavy-duty pipe wrench, which was virtually break-proof. The firm has had a lot of other technical firsts since then.

Today, over 70 million wrenches and 55 years later, Ridge has more than 1,600 employees worldwide. The company presently turns out over 300 different tools in a wide variety of models under the internationally known Ridgid brand name.

Pride of craft has been the hallmark of The Ridge Tool Company since its inception 55 years ago. The company is also proud of its accomplishment in developing more innovative products than anyone else in the industry. Many were suggested by users of Ridgid tools, professional tradesmen whose livelihoods depend on the capability of their tools.

Among the company's firsts are: a pipe wrench with an unconditionally guaranteed housing, end wrench, threader for four sizes of pipe and conduit with one set of dies, jam-proof threaders, true-centering workholder for threaders and 2½" x 4" reamer.

Other engineering innovations include: an improved power bender, ratchet lever bender, an improved soil pipe assembly tool, axial pipe cutter, blade-type cutter for plastic, an improved groove-bevel-cutoff machine to prepare large-size pipe for welding and mechanical fittings, and a reasonably priced 4"-pipe-capacity threading machine, which is portable and also cuts and reams.

A few years after its formation in Ridgeville, which is a suburb of Cleveland, Ridge moved a few miles west to a larger factory in Elyria. The company has expanded at this location and also has plants in New Philadelphia, Ohio; Erie, Pa.; Bartlesville, Okla., and St. Truiden, Belgium. Ground has been broken for another manufacturing plant in Brazil. There are also sales and warehousing subsidiaries in Australia, England, Denmark, Sweden, Switzerland, Germany, France and Italy. Ridgid products are sold in more than 121 countries.

The Ridge Tool Company became a subsidiary of Emerson Electric Company of St. Louis in May 1966. Emerson is a diversified concern with established marketing bases throughout the world. An 88-year-old firm, listed on the New York Stock Exchange, it has major interests in the manufacture and sale of electrical and electronic products and systems. Emerson chairman, W.R. Persons, is dedicated to a continuing program of carefully planned long-term growth.

At The Ridge Tool Company, continuity of management is underscored by the fact that there have been only four presidents since the firm's beginnings in 1923. The current president, R.C. Baumgartner, believes in the continuing introduction of new products—power-operated as well as hand tools. Innovation was also the aim of Ridge's first chief executive, Carl Ingwer Sr., who founded the company; William Thewes, inventor of the pioneer wrench, and Arthur Smith, then sales manager.

The new pipe wrench established the Ridge reputation early in its history. By 1930, the Ridgid wrench was already headed toward making the old Stillson obsolete. The company was on its way, producing a comprehensive line for the plumbing, heating, electrical, hardware and other industries.

When World War II started, Ridge was already producing the most complete line of hand pipe tools in the country. Its special mission had become defined—to supply quality professional tools to pipe-using industries through distributors in the various industrial areas. Every effort was, and is still being, made to manufacture in-plant the maximum number of materials and parts going into Ridgid products and to subject them to the most rigid inspection and quality controls.

War production snapped up the company's line, and plant facilities were literally bursting at the seams. Little retooling was necessary, because Ridge's normal tool production was urgently needed by the Government.

With the end of the war, Ridge committed itself to the development of power tools and other major products. In 1946, the company made about 29 types of tools in 106 models. By 1963, the product line consisted of more than 80 types of tools in about 200 models. Today, the line has just about quadrupled.

Always priding itself on innovation, the company took off in the 1960's on product diversification, increased engineering development of new products and expansion of the product line through acquisitions.

During 1963 and 1964, the acquisition program began with the addition of Simplex machinists vises and the 805 Condumatic bender. The Kollman Company of Erie, Pa., producers of pipe-and-drain cleaning equipment, became part of Ridge in 1967. Three years later, P&S Engineering Division of Bartlesville, Okla., joined the Ridge group, bringing in its fusion tools for joining plastic pipe.

New Ridge products are being introduced continually to meet the specific needs of customers. A trend toward power tools has become quite noticeable. In the current year, for the first time, Ridgid power tools will nearly outsell Ridgid hand tools, although the latter have rolled up sizable increases. The future may see the conversion of many existing hand tools to power.

Behind the technical accomplishments of The Ridge Tool Company, there has been, from the very beginning, a consistently strong advertising position as the vigorous right arm of sales. The first president of the company, Carl Ingwer Sr., established this hard-hitting program, and it has grown throughout the years.

During the present year, nearly 2,000 advertisements are appearing in about 240 trade and consumer publications, reaching tool users around the globe. Ridge is also participating in well over 100 trade shows and exhibitions worldwide.

The world-famous Ridgid pin-up calendar in four colors is the company's most important single promotion. A total of 600,000 copies is produced every two years and distributed globally to customers.

The calendar was started in 1936 when it was adorned only by black-and-white photos of tools. Added later were drawings of pretty girls by George Petty and other well-known artists. Photographs of models and Ridge tools were introduced in 1959.

For the last 15 years, the beautiful young women have been photographed for the Ridgid calendar by Hollywood lensman Peter Gowland. There's barely a shop in the various industries, using the company's tools, that doesn't display the calendar. And that's only one of the beauties of Ridge's golden story.

# # #

This one is long—five pages—but it's written as a magazine article, titled simply, "70 Million Wrenches." Several editors used major portions of it, almost verbatim, while others retained it for reference. The backgrounder was distributed with a brief note. It also was used throughout the year as an accompaniment to news releases and other mailings which were dated. Hence, the backgrounder was not dated.

From: PR agency's name, address and phone

For: Lexington School for the Deaf
For Immediate Release, Jan. 26

LEXINGTON SCHOOL FOR THE DEAF ELECTS PRESIDENT

Robert I. Weissmann, a New York attorney, has been elected president of the Lexington School for the Deaf, Queens, N.Y.

A member of the New York law firm of Wien Lane & Malkin, Mr. Weismann was graduated from Columbia University School of Law and Columbia College. He was an editor of the *Columbia Law Review* and a member of Phi Beta Kappa.

Mr. Weismann, his wife and four children live in Scarsdale, N.Y.; he is active in several community organizations. A volunteer fireman, he was president of Fairview Engine Co. No. 1, Greenburgh, N.Y.

Located on a $10-million campus in Jackson Heights, the 106year-old Lexington School for the Deaf provides speech and hearing services for infants, children and adults; operates a preschool, nursery school, elementary school and high school, and conducts research, teacher training and other programs. Mr. Weissmann succeeds Daniel Jacobson, who was president for four years.

* * *

Personnel Release *One of the most common types of news release is the announcement of personnel—appointed, elected, promoted.*

The format generally is:

First paragraph—identify the person, position and organization.

Second paragraph—professional or business data about the person.

Third paragraph—personal details, including hometown and family.

Fourth paragraph—information about the company or organization.

From: PR agency's name, address and phone

TIMME FAKE FUR AND OTHER FABRICS SHOWN IN
FASHION SHOW

A wardrobe of several fake fur coats is replacing the old status symbol of a single fur coat, according to E.F. Timme.

A fashion show of a variety of "Timme-tation" coats, which resemble wild animal furs, was shown today (Thursday) at a luncheon at the St. Regis Hotel in New York. "In addition to the ecological and price advantages, Timme fabrics enable fashionable men and women to be more individualistic than in the days when fur coat selection was limited by nature," said William E. Roschen Jr., chairman of the board of E.F. Timme & Son, Inc.

The event, attended by over 100 apparel and home furnishings manufacturers, was to show the versatility of Timme woven pile fabrics, which resemble fur in texture and design. Though high-pile fabrics remain Timme's largest product, there is great potential growth now in warp knits, with increases also projected for knitted pile fabrics.

Warp knits, which used to be used primarily for low-priced underwear, now are being produced with textured and spun yarns which are used in a variety of high-quality slacks, blouses, dresses, jackets, rainwear, room dividers and upholstery. Many creative double-knit apparel manufacturers now are working with warp knit fabrics as a result of new manufacturing and yarn technology, noted Mr. Roschen.

Top-line models of General Motors and Ford automobiles feature Timme velour upholstery, and many furniture manufacturers are using various Timme fabrics.

The fashion show featured women's garments made by Darmar Coats, Dubrowsky & Joseph, Louis Shansky, Town Talk Coat and Charles Weinstein Coats (Weatherbee Coats); men's garments by Avente Associates and Chief Apparel; childrens garments by Rainbow Girl, and slippers by Alta and Mart Ray. Each guest received a Timme stuffed tiger.

The event included an excerpt from "Wild Africa," a one-hour special to be sponsored exclusively by Timme on Saturday (Sept. 8) on WNBC-TV in New York. The color film, produced by John Livingston and directed by Bill Banting, was made in East African parks and game preserves. Elephants, zebras, hyenas, cheetahs and other wild animals are shown, with stress on their environmental and ecological interdependence.

Harold Levine, president of Levine, Huntley, Schmidt, advertising agency for Timme, described the fall advertising campaign and showed the new television commercials for Timme fabrics.

Founded in 1895, E.F. Timme & Son is a privately owned

company with over 1400 employees. Executive offices are in New York, the principal manufacturing facility is in Wilmington, North Carolina, and other plants are in Torrington, Connecticut, and Cape May, New Jersey. The 138,000-sq.-ft. plant in New Jersey is the newest and now is producing large quantities of warp knit fabrics.

* * *

GROWTH OF MONMOUTH AND OCEAN COUNTIES HAILED BY SPEAKERS AT LUNCHEON CELEBRATING EXPANSION OF MONMOUTH SHOPPING CENTER

Monmouth and Ocean Counties are the fastest-growing counties in New Jersey.

State, county and local government officials and other speakers all emphasized this theme at a luncheon today (Wednesday) to celebrate the start of the expansion program of Monmouth Shopping Center. The shopping center, located in Eatontown in Monmouth County, serves the shopping needs of the increasingly large population in the area.

About 200 community leaders, government officials and business executives attended a luncheon at the Old Orchard Inn. Speakers were Reverend Robert Reed of the First Presbyterian Church in Eatontown; Herbert E. Werner, mayor of the Borough of Eatontown; John L. Keaveney, president of the Monmouth-Ocean Development Council; Ronald Heymann, commissioner of the New Jersey Department of Labor and Industry, and Charles Leibler, vice president of Arlen Development Company.

Commissioner Heymann noted that Monmouth and Ocean Counties are among the fastest-growing counties in the country. Monmouth County is projected by the Regional Plan Association as the third-largest gainer in population among the 31 counties in the metropolitan New York area.

Other data also indicate the need for a major shopping center in the area. For example, Monmouth County is third in the state in issuance of residential building permits. The two counties have a great deal of new industry and are tops as a resort area. Tourism and resorts rank among the top three industries in the state.

Commissioner of the Department of Labor and Industry since 1971, Ronald Heymann previously was director of the Division of Motor Vehicles and before that was an executive with the New Jersey Telephone Company.

John Keaveney congratulated Arlen for its commitment to the future of the area and discussed the social, economic, tax, employment and other benefits of the expansion of the Monmouth Shopping Center. Mr. Keaveney, who is assistant

123

vice president in charge of industrial relations at the Central Jersey Bank and Trust Company in Freehold, previously was in charge of this area for the Federal Bureau of Investigation. He retired from the F.B.I. in 1965, after 25 years of service.

The expanded shopping center, a $25-million project, is expected to have annual sales in excess of $120 million after its third year of expansion. Focal point of the center is a two-level, enclosed mall which will be divided into small park-like areas with naturally lighted, landscaped, interior courts. The existing 610,000-square-foot shopping center, which includes Bamberger's and Alexander's department stores, will be increased more than two-fold, to over 1,500,000 square feet of leasable area on a 105-acre landscaped site, with parking for over 7200 cars.

* * *

For Immediate Release

GOV. THOMSON TO ATTEND NEWINGTON PLAZA GROUNDBREAKING, ENCLOSED MALL SHOPPING CENTER TO INCLUDE FIELDS AND WARD STORES

Governor Meldrim Thomson and more than 50 civic officials and business leaders will participate in groundbreaking ceremonies to be held Thursday, May 24, at Newington Plaza in Newington, N.H.

The 400,000-square-foot enclosed mall shopping center is being built on a 63-acre site adjacent to the city of Portsmouth, in the southeast portion of New Hampshire and bordering on Maine and Massachusetts. The location is at the intersections of Gosling Road with the highly trafficked Spaulding Turnpike and Routes 4 and 16. The shopping center will be easily accessible to the hundreds of thousands of shoppers in the tristate area.

Newington Plaza will feature an enclosed air-conditioned and heated mall, with J.M. Fields and Montgomery Ward department stores, each approximately 100,000 square feet. The Fields store, presently in operation, will be expanded by more than 30 percent. Montgomery Ward will open later this year. The project, when completed in 1974, will include a 30,000-square-foot Pantry Pride supermarket and approximately 45 stores inthe enclosed mall, thus constituting the largest center for shopping in the region.

Newington Plaza is being developed by Arlen Development Company, a division of Arlen Realty & Development Corp., New York, and U.S. Gypsum Urban Development Company, a subsidiary of United States Gypsum Co., Chicago. Arlen owns and manages more than 200 shopping centers in the country, including several in New England.

The architect is Robert Kahn Associates of New York. Raymond Keyes Associates of Elmsford, N.Y., is site engineer.

The enclosed mall will include a decor and amenities designed for an enjoyable shopping experience, plus on-site parking for more than 2500 cars. Every store will be only a short distance from the parking areas.

For Immediate Release

MAYOR CASCAES AND OTHER FREEHOLD OFFICIALS TO ATTEND GROUNDBREAKING AT WEMROCK FARM

The start of construction of Wemrock Farm, a 1400-unit residential community to be built on a 180-acre site in Freehold, N.J. will be celebrated at groundbreaking ceremonies on Saturday morning (Oct. 27).

The one- and two-story condominium homes will be built in clusters on a site renowned for its shade trees and natural beauty. Entrances are on Route 537, near the Greater Freehold Area Hospital, and also on Wemrock Road, south of Freehold.

Wemrock Farm will be developed by Gene A. Genola Company, Inc., Shrewsbury, N.J., managing partner, and Arfree Realty Corp., N.Y., financial partner in the joint venture. Participants at the groundbreaking event will be Gene A. Genola, president; Gerard Primavera, executive vice president, and William H. Weimer, vice president, all of the Gene A. Genola Company, and Joel H. Kagan, vice president of Arfree Realty Corp., a subsidiary of Arlen Realty & Development Corp.

An engraved commemorative shovel will be presented to Romeo Cascaes, Mayor of Freehold. After the groundbreaking, a luncheon for local and county officials will be held at the American Hotel in Freehold.

Wemrock Farm will be a planned adult community, with a nine-hole golf course, a 15-acre nature preserve, picinc areas, fish-stocked lake, swimming pool, tennis courts and other recreational facilities. A community center will provide extensive hobby equipment and large areas for movies, games, dances and meetings. The architect is Beyer-Blinder-Belle, New York.

"The historic flavor and magnificent natural beauty of the scenic countryside will be preserved," noted Mr. Genola, "and will be enhanced with the addition of a variety of shade trees, gardens and landscaping."

The traditional-style, pitched-roof homes will feature an extensive array of convenience items, including central air conditioning, individual electric heating, smoke and fire alarms, master TV antenna and other "carefree, contemporary features." Most will have private entrance, patio and garage.

125

News releases about speeches, fashion shows, product demonstrations, store openings, facility dedications, ground-breakings and other events generally must be prepared prior to the event. However, the texts of speeches, names of participants, numbers of guests and all, or almost all, other data can be obtained prior to the event.

Thus, a news release can be written in past tense *for distribution at the event and afterward. If necessary (though it rarely is), changes can be made at the event.*

Five examples of this type of news release are reproduced here. The Timme and Monmouth releases were prepared prior to the events (luncheons) and distributed to media at the event and by mail and messenger after the event.

The Newington Plaza and Wemrock Farm releases were distributed prior *to the events. After the events, the releases were slightly modified, changed to past tense and distributed with photos taken at the event.*

From: PR agency's name, address and phone

For: Parfums Hermes

Exclusive in Your City

For Immediate Release, Dec. 5

THE PERFECT PERSONAL GIFT FOR CHRISTMAS

A Christmas gift problem that bothers many men and women is how to find a gift that is truly personal and special. We all look for that distinctive gift that will let the recipient feel that he or she is someone special, and this is our way of showing it.

Is there a perfect personal gift which is not too intimate, doesn't require a knowledge of size and is always welcomed even by the person who has everything?

The answer, of course, is perfume and companion fragrance products. You can't go wrong, and, yet, the dazzling array of different types of fragrances and prices makes the decision more than mere snap judgment.

This year, the choice is easier and more exciting, because there are several new products which recently have been

—more—

The Parfums Hermes release, marked Exclusive in Your City, *included the name and address of the department store carrying the product.*

From: PR agency's name, address and phone

For: Parfums Hermes

For Immediate Release

FRENCHMAN OFFERS VALENTINE'S DAY ADVICE FOR LOVERS

All the world loves a lover, and Valentine's Day is a good time to think about famous lovers.

Valentine's Day thoughts often turn to fantasies about being Romeo or Juliet, Tristan or Isolde, Jenifer Cavilleri or Oliver Barrett III, forgetting the tragedies involved with each and only remembering the completeness of their love that has been retold throughout the pages of literature.

Of course, love and tragedy often are as intertwined as pleasure and pain. St. Valentine not only has become the patron of lovers but, more important, the helper of those unhappily in love. His feast day stems from the pagan festival associated with love which occurred in the middle of February.

Of even greater inspiration to lovers on this day are those fairy-tale settings with real-life lovers, such as a prince or princess who marries a "true love" and lives happily ever after. We have seen this fantasy come true in the lives of Prince Rainier and Grace Kelly, the Maharajah of Sikkim and Hope Cooke, and the Duke and Duchess of Windsor. These couples romantically fit the cliche, "and they lived happily ever after," and are more satisfying than the bittersweet romances of fiction.

One definition of a lover is, "a complete person," and on Valentine's Day we try to make that someone special in our life feel complete. Traditionally, this message is conveyed through greeting cards, candy, flowers and, of course, perfume.

The House of Hermes, world-renowned for its handcrafted fashion accessories and scarves, now has a complete line of fragrances—Caleche for women and Equipage for men. "Our fragrances have been created for the complete person and can say on this Valentine's Day that you are special and complete in every way," states Xavier Guerrand-Hermes, head of the American operations of the House of Hermes.

The French are considered by many to be experts on the subject of love, and, according to Mr. Guerrand-Hermes, "In the past, the general rule for fragrances was, the stronger the scent the better. However, lovers no longer want a scent that will attract attention, but rather one that is subtle enough to tell everyone that they are complete and, yes, even in love."

Equipage, which literally means "complete," is the first French fragrance for men to be introduced as a complete line in the United States. Caleche, a distinctive perfume signature, was originally worn by only the most elegant fashion leaders, the kind of women others like to copy. But today, the Caleche wearer is any woman who recognizes quality by instinct. It's rich, sophisticated, very well-bred.

If, on this Valentine's Day, you want to say to someone, "for me you are complete," a gift of fine fragrance can make this statement.

About that statement, "All the world loves a lover," it was written by Elbert Hubbard, an American author and publisher around the turn of the century, who wrote "A Message to Garcia," about an incident in the Spanish-American War. Had he lived today, Mr. Hubbard probably would have been a friend of Mr. Guerrand-Hermes, because they certainly shared many values. For example, Mr. Hubbard founded an artist colony in upstate New York where he operated a shop specializing in handcrafted items.

As for the balance of our love history lesson, let's return to St. Valentine. Our history books generally refer to the Roman priest who died in the third century.

Actually, there were quite a few saints named Valentine. The most celebrated are the two martyrs whose festivals fall on the 14th of February.

The day used to be an occasion to send anonymous greetings and gifts to loved ones, but anonymity has gone the way of handmade lace hearts, and February 14 is sort of an unofficial "day of affection" in many countries. In the United States, Arizona is sometimes called the Valentine state. The explanation is simply that Arizona was the 48th state to be admitted into the Union, on February 14, 1912.

Valentine's Day has a special significance in Colorado, Iowa, Ohio and Oklahoma, as there is a city named Loveland in each of these states.

But, you don't have to live in a special place to celebrate Valentine's Day. You just need a special person.

# # #

Holiday Story   *Looking for a news peg? Look at the calendar. Your company or organization surely must have some kind of tie-in or relationship with:*

The New Year, famous Americans such as Washington and Lincoln, Valentine's Day, Christmas and other holidays, anniversaries and past, current and forthcoming events. The Hermes release required some literary research in order to tie in a very commercial angle with a holiday. It's still quite commercial, but logical for women's pages and broadcasters.

From: Charles Leibler
         Arlen Shopping Centers Company
         888 Seventh Avenue, New York 10019
         (212) 333-2209

Eatontown: Richard Weismann, (201) 542-0333

For Immediate Release, Dec. 6

TEENAGERS CAN BECOME MONMOUTH SHOPPING CENTER CONSTRUCTION ENGINEERS

Boys and girls in this area can become Monmouth Shopping Center Construction Engineers.

Youngsters do not have to know physics, mathematics or other technical subjects to pass the unusual examination.

Applicants, up to the age of 16, only have to study a four-page booklet about the Monmouth Shopping Center in Eatontown. The "cram course" booklet describes the expansion construction now going on at the shopping center, located at Route 35 in Eatontown. The expanded center, which will feature an enclosed mall and five major department stores, will be one of the largest in the country.

After studying the booklet, junior engineers may take the examination on the first Saturday morning of each month. The first test will be given Saturday, January 5, at 11 a.m., in the Civic Auditorium at Monmouth Shopping Center. Those who pass the 10-question exam will receive a T-shirt and other items, including the unusual title, Monmouth Shopping Center Construction Engineer.

The study booklet can be obtained at the Monmouth Shopping Center management office and also at the Ground Round Restaurant at the center.

# # #

Local News Release *The same news release often is sent to local and national media. In this case, a local (New Jersey) contact and phone number was added to the national (New York) contact.*
The booklet described in the release was appended.

For Immediate Release, Oct. 9

HAHNE'S SIGNS LEASE AT MONMOUTH SHOPPING CENTER

Hahne's will start construction in March of a two-level, 160,000-square-foot department store at Monmouth Shopping Center in Eatontown, N.J.

The store will be the chain's fifth in New Jersey. Other Hahne's stores now are in operation in Newark, Westfield, Montclair and Livingston. The architect for the new store is Hamby, Kennerly, Slomanson & Smith, New York.

The lease was signed this week by Arthur O'Day, of

129

Associated Dry Goods Corp., parent company of Hahne's, and Charles Leibler, vice president of U.S.I.F. Wynnewood Corporation, owner of Monmouth Shopping Center. Mr. Leibler stated that site work has already started for the modernization and expansion of the Monmouth Shopping Center.

Bamberger's and Alexander's now are in operation, and Hahne's will be the first of three new department stores to be built at Monmouth Shopping Center. The existing 600,000-square-foot shopping center will be expanded to 1,500,000 square feet and be situated on a 105-acre site. Monmouth Shopping Center is located on Routes 35 and 36, and the Garden State Parkway Spur in Eatontown, New Jersey.

# # #

Trade News Release   *Lots of facts, but not padded, and fits on one page. Ideal for trade publications and also for business and real estate editors of local newspapers. Useful (and economical) also for distribution within the companies and to customers (in this case, prospective tenants).*

Submitted on PR agency's letterhead

Dear Editor:

Colonial Penn Group is an organization of companies specializing in insurance, travel and temporary employment programs for specific customer groups, especially older persons.

A pioneer in the mass marketing of life, accident and health, and automobile insurance, Colonial Penn is a consumer-oriented direct marketing and service operation. Thousands of applications, claims and questions are processed at company headquarters each day.

More than one third of all employees in the insurance operation are directly concerned with answering customer questions by letter, telephone or personal contact.

Despite the system for handling policy-owner questions and complaints, errors and delays may sometimes occur.

If a question involving Colonial Penn or any of its subsidiaries is directed to you, please let us know. We'll help you get the answers you need or direct you to someone who can.

Further information on the company and its services is outlined in the enclosed fact sheet. The index cards will enable you to locate the appropriate spokesman. Please keep them on file, and contact us whenever we can be of service.

Sincerely,
Gerald M. Goldberg

Fact Sheet

Colonial Penn Group specializes in insurance, travel and employment services for specific customer groups, especially older persons.

Established in 1958, Colonial Penn Group is now a major factor in a market constituted by millions of American men and women who are 55 years of age and over.

The Group's insurance subsidiaries provide older persons insurance services which include life, accident and health, and auto coverage.

Colonial Penn Group's Grand Circle travel companies operate group tours thoughout the world, serving the important leisure-time needs of older Americans.

Colonial Penn markets insurance, travel and employment services to members of large national and membership associations, including the National Retired Teachers Association and the American Association of Retired Persons.

Major companies of Colonial Penn Group, Inc., are Colonial Penn Life Insurance Company; Colonial Penn Insurance Company; Colonial Penn Franklin Insurance Company; Intramerica Life Insurance Company; Colonial Penn Travel Services, Inc.; Mature Temps Inc.; National Association Plans, Inc.; Group Association Plans, Inc., and Colonial Penn Group Data Corp.

National Headquarters: 5 Penn Center Plaza
Philadelphia, Pennsylvania 19103
(215) 854-8000

Vice President-Public Relations:
Leslie Nash, (215) 854-8282

Public Relations Representative:
Richard Weiner, Inc.
888 Seventh Ave.
New York, N.Y. 10019
(212) 582-7373

INSURANCE
(older persons)

Colonial Penn Group, Inc., 5 Penn Center Plaza, Philadelphia, Pa. 19103

(215) 854-8000

Colonial Penn Group is a pioneer in serving the health, accident, automobile owner and life insurance needs of the 39 million American men and women who are age 55 and over.

For Information, contact:

Leslie Nash, V.P.   —   Public Relations
(215) 854-8282

NYC Press Contact   —   Richard Weiner, Inc.
(212) 582-7373

RETIREMENT

Colonial Penn Group, Inc., 5 Penn Center Plaza, Philadelphia, Pa. 19103

(215) 854-8000

Colonial Penn Group is a pioneer in serving the health, accident, automobile owner and life insurance needs of the 39 million American men and women who are age 55 and over.

For Information, contact:

Leslie Nash, V.P.   —   Public Relations
(215) 854-8282

NYC Press Contact   —   Richard Weiner, Inc.
(212) 582-7373

NOTE TO EDITORS: This copy of a recent news release is included as an indication of material issued by Colonial Penn. If you have not been receiving our releases, and would like to, please let us know.

From: PR agency's name, address and phone

AUTO INSURANCE WITH NO AGE LIMIT OFFERED TO OLDER PERSONS

PHILADELPHIA—Older motorists in 47 states and the District of Columbia have been assured of continued automobile insurance coverage without any age limit, as the result of new insurance provisions introduced by Colonial Penn Insurance Company, according to an announcement by Robert Pollack, president.

Mr. Pollack announced that Colonial Penn will guarantee to continue insurance coverage for policyholders over age 50 with no age limit, as long as they hold valid operator's licenses, are not deemed medically unfit to drive by their own physicians and continue to pay premiums. The policy was previously guaranteed renewable to age 80, with yearly renewals thereafter.

"The elimination of age as a factor in continuing auto insurance is based on the good experience the company has had with older drivers in past years," Mr. Pollack said.

Before developing the new provisions, the company analyzed the driving records of 500,000 drivers over age 50. The study showed that older drivers, as a group, average fewer accidents than all other drivers. Age alone is not a factor in continued safe driving, Colonial Penn determined.

Mr. Pollack said this study was supported by National Safety Council statistics, indicating older drivers make up nearly 30 percent of all drivers, but they are involved in only a little over 20 percent of all accidents reported in the country.

Colonial Penn Insurance Company, a subsidiary of Colonial Penn Group, Inc., has been a pioneer in developing insurance for the older driver. It was the first company to guarantee insurance renewable to age 80.

The company also was the first to offer a 10 percent discount to all policyholders who completed the National Safety Council's Defensive Driving Course.

Fact Kit   *This is a type of press kit designed for immediate use and also reference. The Colonial Penn kit contained the company annual report and booklet (not shown here), letter, fact sheet (single-spaced, with several phone numbers), index cards and one news release.*

XAVIER GUERRAND-HERMES

Born and educated in France, 37-year-old Xavier Guerrand-Hermes is director of the House of Hermes in the United States and represents the fifth generation of family involvement in the ownership and management of the prestigious 141-year-old Paris-based firm.

133

Mr. Guerrand-Hermes was graduated from Ecole des Roches and the Sorbonne in Paris, and he is an accomplished sportsman whose love of horses regularly took him to Ireland for the annual Dublin Horse Show.

At school, he concentrated on the arts and business administration, and participated in such sports as tennis, skiing, riding, hockey and rugby.

When he came to the United States in 1965, he did graduate work in business at Columbia University and New York University.

He is an avid art collector and owns an extensive selection of 18th-century furniture and an art-noveau collection that has been exhibited in Paris.

Mr. Guerrand-Hermes divides his time equally between New York and France, maintaining a Park Avenue apartment two blocks from the House of Hermes headquarters in the United States, an apartment in Paris and a villa in Cannes, overlooking the sea.

He is an enthusiastic world traveler who regularly journeys to lesser-known countries to become acquainted firsthand with their customs and cultural heritage.

Like his father, Jean Guerrand-Hermes, who is the chairman of the board of Parfums Hermes and on the board of directors of the House of Hermes, Xavier is a highly respected gourmet and wine connoisseur and a partial owner of vinyards in Bordeaux and, until recently, California.

He is a member of the Wine and Food Society in New York, and as a bachelor has become what he terms "an inventive cook who prefers the artistry of creation in the kitchen rather than the practical cleaning up of the aftermath."

January, 1978

For additional information: Richard Weiner, Inc.
Xavier Guerrand-Hermes public relations
Hermes 888 Seventh Avenue
745 Fifth Avenue New York, N.Y. 10019
New York, N.Y. 10022 (212) 582-7373
(212) 759-7585 home: (212) 799-1197

Biography *Various types of formats are used for biographies, depending on the person, type of occupation and media. This biography of Xavier Guerrand-Hermes weaves the vital facts into an article about his hobbies and other interests, and is useful as a "backgrounder" for interviews.*

This type of biography should be sent to radio and television broadcasters and other interviewers in an attempt to elicit an interview and, then, when the interview is scheduled, for reference by the interviewer.

Note the inclusion of a date, telephone number, including home phone.

Biographies should be reissued annually and sent to media librarians and others who are likely to file such information. In some cases, a list of publications, performances, positions or other resume-type data is appended, as well as a fact sheet with names of parents, children and other facts compiled in a "Who's Who" format.

The final use for biographical articles and fact sheets is for obituaries, which generally must be prepared and distributed very quickly, which is one more reason for through preparation of biographies of all key individuals in an organization.

What do most American women *really* think about love, sex and romance? In what areas do they adamantly cling to tradition? Is there a porn backlash? What kind of men do most women really want? What kind of woman do they want to be, wish they were?

Janet Dailey has some interesting answers to those questions— for she has written 28 Harlequin Books, *the world's bestselling paperbacks*. The information enclosed will give you an idea of how astonishingly popular Harlequin Books are. Last year, Harlequin *sold* 80 million books—over 50 million in the United States.

While women enjoy historical and Gothic romances, the sales of Harlequin Books—all contemporary romances—far eclipse any other form of romantic novel. In the U.S. alone, 11 million women read Harlequin Books.

Janet's biography is enclosed. In it you will note that she and her husband are touring the United States seeking new locations for Harlequin novels. They will be in _____ .

We think Janet Dailey could give you an exceptional interview. (Attached are some possible questions you might like to put to her.) She is, not incidentally, an extremely attractive and charming young woman.

Sincerely,

_____

Harlequin Books

Possible interview questions:

There is so much talk about women and careers, women becoming independent of men, yet every Harlequin novel depicts a very traditional romance with a "masterful" man. What happened to women's lib? **135**

The feminist position seems to be that marriage is only one—and maybe the wrong—alternative for today's woman. Yet all Harlequin books end with the man and woman getting married. Aren't you ignoring the impact of feminism on American women?

You are very much a "career woman," by anybody's standards. Yet your novels are concerned solely with love and marriage. Are you being straight with your readers?

All Harlequin heroines are virgins—and no sex takes place before marriage. What happened to the sexual revolution?

What kind of woman reads Harlequin books?

What questions, advice or criticisms do you most often get from your readers?

Letter to Media   *There are as many different styles of "pitch letters" as news releases. Here's one in which the subject (romance) and the client (Harlequin Books) are mentioned before the person who is being suggested for an interview. The "form letter" had a blank space for insertion of the city and dates in which the author (Janet Dailey) would be available for interviews.*

The enclosures included a photo and biography of the interviewee, one or more of her Harlequin books, a backgrounder about the publisher and a list of "possible interview questions."

This list often is appreciated by broadcast interviewers but, as with all publicity materials, must be used with discretion. For example, broadcasters sometimes are interested in seeing clippings (from other cities or national media) or in knowing about programs on which the person previously appeared.

MONDAY / SEPT. 12

BOSTON, MASS. Arrive anytime Sunday. Reservations at Hotel Colonnade.

Good Morning! Limo pickup at 7:45 A.M. Check out of hotel.

8:30 A.M.	WCVB-TV (ABC) Five TV Place, Needham (617) 449-0400 GOOD DAY Thea Chadow, contact. Hosts: John Willis & Janet Langhart.	Live eight- to ten-minute interview. Show will arrange for limo service for pickup at hotel and delivery to next appointment.

10:00 A.M.	BOSTON HERALD AMERICAN 300 Harrison Ave. (617) 426-3000 Peggy Saunders, women's editor.	Interview for a Sunday feature. Photographer from newspaper will photograph you.
12:00 Noon	WBZ-TV (NBC) FIRST FOUR NEWS 1170 Soldiers Field Road (617) 787-7018 Darryl Rehr, contact and host.	Tape six-minute interview. Ask receptionist for Darryl Rehr. Receptionist will call taxi for Boston Globe interview in Dorchester. You'll have time for lunch.
2:30 P.M.	BOSTON GLOBE 135 Morrissey Blvd. (617) 929-2811 Bruce McCabe, film and literary columnist and interviewer.	Interview will be held at office. Ask guard in lobby for Bruce McCabe. Call taxi to next interview in Allston (20-minute ride).
4:00 P.M.	WGBH Radio 125 Western Ave. (617) 492-2777, Ext. 561 PANTECHNICON Greg Fitzgerald, contact. Hosts: Elinor Stout and Bill Cavness	Tape 30-minute interview. Ask receptionist in lobby for Greg Fitzgerald.
REMINDER: BRING BOOKS!		Call taxi to airport. Eastern Shuttle to New York leaves every hour on the hour.

Interview *This actual schedule was given to an author for a day in*
Schedule *Boston—two TV interviews, two daily newspapers and a radio*
program. It indeed was a good day, and it was made better
because the publicist included details about interviewers,
transportation and locations.

MEDIA GLOSSARY

Jess Wolf, director of publications of the International Council of Shopping Centers, published the following list of common newspaper, radio and television terms as part of a public relations manual for ICSC members. Of course, you can be an effective publicist without knowing the meaning of lobster trick, double truck or other special language of printers, journalists and broadcasters. However, it can help in conversations with media people to have some familiarity with their technical vocabulary.

Newspaper Terms

ADD: new copy added to a story already written
ADVANCE: news story of a future event
ALIVE: copy still available for use
A.M.: morning newspaper
ANGLE: a particular viewpoint or emphasis played up in the story
ART: illustrations
BOIL: reduce the copy
BREAK (as a noun): time when news is available
BREAK (as a verb): to make news available
BULLETIN: late news printed before the lead of a story
BY-LINE: line containing the name of the reporter
CANNED COPY: syndicate or publicity copy
C.G.O.: copy to be held or used at another time (Can Go Over)
CLIP SHEET: a series of publicity matter in sheet form
COPY DESK: where copy is read, edited, headlined
COPY EDITOR (copyreader): staff member who reads, corrects, edits copy
CUT: an engraving, line or half-tone
DATELINE: line indicating date of medium's publication

DAY SIDE: daytime staff of paper

DEAD: copy or type that no longer has any use

DEADLINE: specified time when copy is due

DOG WATCH: period after last edition during which small staff watches for late stories

DOUBLE TRUCK: an advertisement on two facing pages including the gutter

DUMMY: a scaled layout of a newspaper page showing positions of ads and stories

DUPES: carbon copies of manuscripts

EDITORIALIZE: to inject opinions in a news story

END MARK: symbol (usually #) indicating end of story

FACSIMILE: reproduction of news medium and its distribution by radio

FAKE: fabrication of news story

FILLER: copy prepared in advance for use when space permits

FLIMSY: duplicate copy

FLOP: to turn a negative so that left and right hand sides of photo or art are transposed

FUTURE: record of coming event, usually kept in a book

F.Y.I.: for your information

GALLEY PROOF: a proof of the type as it comes from the composing room

GHOST WRITER: someone employed to write under another's name

GLOSSY PRINT: high gloss finish on photo print

GUIDELINE: part of headline written on news copy to relate the two when type is set and paper being made up. In radio it is a short identification of a news story.

GUTTER: blank space or inner margin between facing pages

HANDOUT: news release

HALFTONE: reproduction of a continuous tone artwork, usually a photograph with the image created by size and proximity of dots

INTRO: opening portion of a story

KILL: to remove portions from story or to destroy type

LAST WATCH: staff to handle late copy or produce last edition

LEAD: opening paragraph or paragraphs of a story

LEG MAN: reporter who gathers news and relays to rewrite man

LOCALIZE: to emphasize local angle

LOBSTER TRICK: early morning working hours

MAT, MATRIX: papier-mache mold into which molten metal is poured to form duplicate of original

MONITORING: listening to a radio or television program

MORE: written at bottom of page of copy to indicate that additional copy is to come

MORGUE: library or reference department

MOVE: sending a story out over news wires

MUST: executive order indicating that copy must be printed

OBIT: obituary
OPTIONAL COPY: extra stories available if needed
PAD: to lengthen a story without adding substance
PERSONAL: news item about persons
P.M.: afternoon newspaper
PONY SERVICE: summary of press association news obtained by telephone
PRECEDE: additional news often set ahead of lead
RELEASE: date at which news copy can be used
REWRITE MAN: reporter who rewrites copy or takes story over telephone from a leg man
ROUNDUP: summary of news, can be general or in a specific area
RUNNING STORY: continuing story lasting several days
SACRED COW: favored subjects or material
SCOOP: news story exclusive with one medium
SECTIONAL STORY: long story appearing in sections
SHIRTTAIL: short story which follows a related item
SIDEBAR: short news items or features adjacent to a related story
SLANTING: stressing certain aspects of news
SLOT: section of copy desk where editor or chief copyreader sits
SLUG: word identifying news story
SOB STUFF: stories with emotional or sentimental appeal
SQUIB: very short news item
STRINGER: correspondent for newspaper, usually out-of-town
SUMMARY LEAD: lead that presents highlights of news
SYNDICATE: company that sells various kinds of copy to media
THIRTY: indication of end of news story
TIME COPY: copy that is available for use at any time

Radio and Television Terms

AD LIB: unscripted, spur-of-the-moment comment
ADJACENCIES: commercials placed next to certain programming
AFFILIATE: independently owned station that provides some of its time to network programs; remainder is programmed locally
AUDIO: the sound part of radio or television
BEEPER: a telephone interview recorded on tape. Telephone circuit emits a regular beep sound to inform parties that they are being recorded.
BRIDGE: a few words tying one element of news to another
CALL LETTERS: the station's name. Most stations east of the Mississippi have call letters beginning with "W"; west of the Mississippi, call letters usually begin with "K."
CART: cartridge case containing magnetic tape
CLIP: an edited film story. Can also be an audio clip of tape.
CONTINUITY: program copy; also can be copy for commercials

141

CUE: a signal in words or signs

CUTAWAY: a short piece of film usually placed between two scenes of the same person or locale

DOPE SHEET: the paper on which the cameraman writes story and film information

DRIVE TIME: the morning and afternoon hours when listeners drive to and from work

FEATURE: a story, usually human interest, whose news value is not especially timely, as distinct from HARD NEWS or COPY, which has timeliness

HEAD SHOT: a still photo of a person's head and shoulders

INDEPENDENT: station not affiliated with a network

LINEUP: arrangements of items in a newscast

LONG SHOT (LS): camera view which takes in the full scene of an event

MOS (Man-on-Street): interviewing of the public

NETWORK: a program service supplying news to affiliated stations

NEWSCAST: straight news program on radio or television

NEWS EDITOR: staff member who rewrites, edits and supervises news program on radio or television

PAD COPY: news stories not scheduled, but available if needed

PICKUP: point at which a program is picked up for airing

PREEMPT: to replace a regular program with something of greater interest or timeliness

REMOTE: a broadcast from a place other than the station's studio

RUNNING TIME: the time from the start of a program or segment

SECS: seconds

STANDUPPER: a report at the scene of an event with the camera focused on the reporter

STILL: a photograph, map or drawing

TEASE: a bit of news preceding the newscast; also an announcement of an upcoming story

TIGHT SHOT: close-up scene

UPDATE: a new version of a previously covered story

VIDEO: the pictorial portion of a television broadcast

VOICE OVER (VO): speech by a newscaster or announcer over films or cards

More broadcast terms are on page 146.

FILM GLOSSARY

A publicist should have a familiarity with the technical production aspects of printing, motion pictures, radio and other media. You don't have to be a printer, for example, to know the difference between offset and letterpress, and a publicist should know this. The jargon of filmmakers often is more foreign to publicists than is the vocabulary of print media people. Michael Rosenthal, a film producer who works with many public relations clients, has compiled a Film Glossary. The complete list of terms can be obtained from MRA Communicators, Inc., 565 Fifth Ave., New York, 10017. Following are a few excerpts:

ANSWER PRINT: the first approved print of a color film which is the standard for all prints made later

BREAKDOWN: an analysis of costs involved in putting together a film including expenses for crew, locations, film processing, etc.

CLOSE-UP: a shot which is taken of a subject revealing the face or face and part of the shoulders only

COMPOSITE PRINT: a positive print of a film that has both sound and picture

CROSSCUT: to edit the shots of two or more scenes together so that bits of each scene are presented

DISSOLVE: progressive blending of the end of one shot into the beginning of the next, produced by the superimposition of a fade-out into a fade-in of equal duration

DUB: simply, to rerecord or to rerecord the original language on the sound track of a film, substituting another language

DUPE NEGATIVE: a negative made from a positive print of a film, or any negative other than the original negative

ESTABLISHING SHOT: in order to acquaint the audience

with the details of the shots to be shown, a longer shot is introduced beforehand.

FADE-IN: a shot that begins in darkness and gradually lightens up to full brightness. In its relation to sound, fade-in can mean the gradual heightening of sound volume.

FADE-OUT: opposite of fade-in

FLASHBACK: repeat of a small part from an earlier scene in a film, either as a reminder to the audience or as a remembrance on the part of one of the characters.

FRAME: one single transparent photograph of the multitude printed on a strip of film

JUMP CUT: cut that breaks continuous time by skipping forward from one part of an action to another, obviously separated from the first by a space of time

LEADER: length of film joined to the beginning of a reel for threading through the camera or projector. Any blank framed film used to join other film. "Academy" leader contains numbers and is used at the beginning of the reel to focus, etc.

LONG SHOT: shot taken far away from a subject

MONTAGE: an assortment of short shots designed to connect lapses of time in a film by indicating the passing of events within it

MOVIOLA: most common trade name for an upright film editing machine

OPTICAL: a special effect used in film such as a fade, dissolve, wipe, etc.

OUT-TAKE: shots not used in a finished film

PAN: camera movement in a horizontal pattern when shooting

RAW STOCK: unexposed or unprocessed film

REACTION SHOT: a shot, usually of a person in a film, showing his response to action or words in the preceding shot

REAR PROJECTION: film projection onto a screen from a projector behind the screen which creates a kind of backdrop to action going on in front of it

REDUCTION PRINT: a print which is narrower than the actual size it was shot in, as in an 8mm print being made from a 16mm negative

RELEASE PRINT: a print of a film that has been screened and approved for general showing

ROUGH CUT: first gathering together of selected takes in the order planned in the script, which is usually then polished by more exact cutting and rearrangement

SHOOTING SCHEDULE: list of shots in the script put in order of what is most convenient to shoot rather than in order of how they appear in the story

STOCK SHOT: shot used in a film that was not shot specifically for that film. This stock footage can be obtained from libraries, etc.

SUPERIMPOSE: to print one shot on top of the other so that

when they are projected on a screen one can be seen through the other

TAKE: during the production, it is one single recording of a shot

WORK PRINT: otherwise known as "dailies," the initial print off the master negative used to assemble the rough cut

RADIO SIGNALS

In an excellent booklet, Radio: Get the Message, by Gary Marx, the National Association of Broadcasters includes the following glossary of signals and terms useful for interviews.

Cue   A signal for you to begin your performance. Usually, the engineer or producer will nod his head in your direction or point directly at you. You may be asked to take your cue from the "on the air" light.

Stand By   A request for you to remain quiet because the performance is about to begin. Your mike may be coming on momentarily. Clear your throat and remove the paper clip or staple from your script.

Time Signal   The number of fingers displayed by the producer represents the number of minutes remaining in the program or program segment.

Stretch   A signal to read more slowly. The non-verbal signal for "stretch" is similar to pulling taffy.

Speed Up   A signal to read more rapidly. The non-verbal "speed up" signal is both hands rotating in a circular motion.

Wrap Up   A signal to close the show. The non-verbal signal is one hand rotating in a circular motion. Bring the program to a conclusion as rapidly as possible.

Louder   With palm up, the hand is raised to signal you to speak a bit more loudly, or for the engineer to increase the intensity of the sound.

Softly   With palm down, the hand is lowered to signal that you should speak a bit more softly.

Cut   A signal, the index finger drawn across the throat, to indicate that the program or spot will stop abruptly. Also refers to the selection you wish to use from a record or tape, such as "Cut 2."

Background When music or sound effects are used to enhance a presentation, they are faded to a lower (background) level.

Up Full Music, voice, or sound effects are heard at full level.

Fade Under Music or sound effects are faded sufficiently to be heard only in the background.

Fade Out Music or sound effects, or even voice, are faded completely out.

Curtain Music is brought up to full level until it reaches its final notes. Or, the end of the program.

Multiple Voice More than one person is heard on the spot or program.

Cow Catcher Comments made even before the introduction of a show to capture attention.

Board Fade The engineer lowers the intensity of music or other sounds.

Body Fade A gradual decrease in intensity caused by physically turning away from the microphone. The technique is sometimes used for transitions.

Balance When both music and voice are used simultaneously, one should not overpower the other. Therefore, a proper "balance" is needed. When two or more persons appear on a program, the engineer will also want to balance the intensity of the voices.

Pot A volume control on the engineer's control panel.

VU Meter A meter on the control board showing the intensity of sounds.

Level An engineer will generally ask you to "give him a level." He is requesting that you speak for a short period of time to allow him to set his controls for the intensity of your voice.

THE PUBLIC RELATIONS LIBRARY

Almost every law office has a library consisting of, at the minimum, several dozen volumes and subscriptions costing a few thousand dollars a year. Major legal departments and law firms often have libraries staffed by reference librarians with six-figure budgets.

Almost all advertising agencies and departments subscribe to the Standard Rate & Data Service and other publications, which generally cost a few thousand dollars a year. Many companies provide office and/or home subscriptions to Advertising Age and other publications to each executive.

It is embarrasing to note that the public relations field is way behind attorneys and advertisers with regard to libraries. Most public relations agencies and departments, including the large prosperous ones, do not have as many public relations books and periodicals as they should. As a result, they often operate without many of the basic tools of our trade.

Compared to law, medicine and other professions, public relations is woefully imprecise. Perhaps these are unfair comparisons. Public relations is young, compared to these professions, and does not have the decades of precedents, decisions, statutes and case histories for guidance.

But thousands of case histories have been published in public relations textbooks and periodicals. It is not necessary for public relations practitioners to reinvent the wheel every time a new problem or project is assigned. Yet, that is the way most of us operate, relying almost entirely on our own experiences or those of our colleagues. It generally works, but it's unnecessary and wasteful.

More shocking is the use of outdated media directories or the operation of a publicity department without *all* types of media directories. This does not mean that it is necessary to purchase every media directory. Some directories are better than others or are specialized in areas which you rarely work or cover the same subjects as in other books.

As with lawyers, you should have access to a university or other library which stocks books which you do not need on a regular basis. Most journalism departments stock public relations reference books or will order them for you. One of the best libraries is at the Public Relations Society of America, 845 Third Avenue, New York.

When you order a reference book, study it carefully, so that you are familiar with the types of data. For example, the Editor & Publisher Year Book is used for its comprehensive information about the editorial personnel of the daily newspapers in the U.S. and Canada. Many regular users are unaware of the gold mine of other data which the book includes, such as advertising rates, newspapers throughout the world, foreign correspondents in the U.S., advertising representatives of U.S. and foreign publications, and advertising and journalism schools, clubs, organizations and awards. Though the price of this annual directory is only $20, many public relations managers try to get by with ordering a new book every two or three years.

Unfortunately, many publicists waste hundreds of dollars in time and mailing costs by sending news releases and other publicity material to nonexistent publications or misaddressed publications. No media directory can be completely accurate and up-to-date, but almost all of the standard directories are extremely reliable and can save time and money many times beyond their cost.

The prices of several long-established media directories have been increased in recent years (along with everything else), and there is a temptation to do without them or make do with the previous edition. Most of the media directories are fairly priced, particularly in view of the vast research required to produce them and their relatively limited market.

Whether you buy a few or all of these media directories, you should be familiar with their contents, attempt to keep them up-to-date, annotate their pages with your personal additions and revisions, and use them "often and well." Several publishers issue supplements and revision sheets. If you use a directory frequently, it is worthwhile to take the time to go through the book and pencil in all additions and changes, rather than inserting the supplement inside the cover.

Your best source for the most comprehensive media information cannot be found in any directory, but rather by reading a current issue of the specific publication or listening to the particular radio or TV station. A few publications provide lists of their editorial personnel.

It is not likely that a public relations agency or department or even a library, college or reference service stocks every one of these dozens of media directories. One of the most frequently asked questions by publicists is, "Which are the one or two best 'all purpose' media directories?"

This directory author surveyed public relations departments and agencies about current and past editions of media directories which they own. Here are the results.

The most "popular" books are Bacon's Publicity Checker, which topped the list, closely followed by Editor & Publisher International Year Book and Ayer Directory of Publications. Other widely owned books are Working Press of the Nation, New York Publicity Outlets and Broadcasting Yearbook.

The public relations agencies generally reported owning more reference books than the public relations departments of companies and associations. More companies than agencies "make do" with last year's, or older, editions of directories, particularly the Broadcasting Yearbook.

It is shocking to see back-issue directories, such as two- and three-year-old editions of Ayer, being used by prominent publicists. Regardless of your prominence and affluence, you probably should be investing more heavily in current editions of all major directories, and keep the books up-to-date and make use of them. Bigger expenditures and greater respect for the tools of the trade can produce substantial efficiencies and economies.

There is one way to save a small amount of money. A few publishers offer prepublication discounts, and, in some cases, a standing order for each new edition is available. Payment with order generally produces a saving in the postage or handling charge, and occasionally discounts are available to purchasers of multiple copies.

If you are not a media buff, and have "average" or minimal publicity needs, can you select a basic publicity library, a sort of five-foot shelf package?

It is impossible to pinpoint the single most indispensable directory. Possibly if a publicist were absolutely restricted to owning only one directory, the choice would be Ayer. However, the choice would depend upon the type of work, and the active publicist cannot function with only one directory.

Incidentally, no single directory is perfect, and there is no such thing as an all-in-one directory for publicists. Ayer is the most comprehensive in the print field, but a comparison of the Washington, D.C., section of Ayer with Hudson's Washington Directory indicates the superiority of the latter specialized book.

Each new edition of the Ayer involves about 100,000 changes in over 22,000 listings of newspapers, magazines and other publications. Though the cost is over $50, this encyclopedic book is so much more than a media directory that it's an indispensable bargain. For example, the dozens of maps enable users to locate over 8500 cities and towns with publications, and thus to target mailings with localized information.

Following is a recommended *"basic"* library of media directories. It should be supplemented by other books and services, in accordance with one's needs and method of operation.

One final note. Any evaluation is not totally objective. This evaluator has two prejudices. First, he's a media directory buff. And, second, the list includes two media directories by this author.

Ayer Directory of Publications
Bacon's Publicity Checker
Broadcasting Yearbook
Editor & Publisher International Year Book
Hudson's Washington News Media Contacts Directory
Literary Market Place
Media News Keys
New York Publicity Outlets
News Bureaus In the U.S.
Party Line
Radio-Television Contact Cards
Syndicated Columnists
TV Publicity Outlets

A description of these 13 books, and about 100 others, is included in the media directory chapter in "Professional's Guide to Public Relations."

Public relations research consists of much more than using media directories.

Research can encompass spending a few hours reading back issues of newspapers, magazines and other publications in a nearby public library. A similar type of background research consists of going through corporate files, publicity scrapbooks and correspondence. This type of research may provide helpful information and clues to problem situations, but this is more in the nature of background briefing rather than exploring new areas.

Too many public relations practitioners rely on their own well-stocked memories and files, and lack basic reference books. Almost every office includes an abridged dictionary as its primary reference book, but even a small publicity operation should consider one or more of the following reference books as being equally essential.

(1) Unabridged Dictionary. There's quite a difference between Merriam-Webster and Random House, as well as distinct variations among other well-known unabridged dictionaries, and purchasers should consider convenience, number of words, style and other factors which are considerably more important than price.

(2) Encyclopedia. A journalistic axiom is "check your facts."

You may not need a complete set of the Encyclopaedia Britannica in your office, but there are several handy, low-cost sources of statistics and other factual data which should be available to you. Take your pick, for example, from among the World Almanac, Information Please Almanac, Reader's Digest Almanac, Hammond Almanac (formerly The New York Times Encyclopedic Almanac) and other low-priced paperbacks.

(3) Word Books. For speech writers and all types of authors, Bartlett's Familiar Quotations, Roget's Thesaurus and other classics not only are indispensable reference sources but also provide reading pleasure. As with all reference books, each edition includes a considerable amount of revisions and new material and usually is preferable to outdated editions.

Very few public relations departments have the space or cataloging resources to keep back issues of The Wall Street Journal and other general publications which they receive. A public relations practitioner should be familiar with one or more public libraries.

In addition to The New York Times Index and The Wall Street Journal Index, the most common "jumping-off point" generally is the Reader's Guide to Periodical Literature. Two other valuable indexes which are not commonly known are the Business Periodical Index and the Funk & Scott Index (business articles, including newsletters and other offbeat sources).

To take advantage of the axiom that "man bites dog" is news, publicists often look for offbeat facts, anecdotes and colorful material. To this end, three useful reference books are Kane's Famous First Facts, The Guinness Book of Records and old editions of encyclopedias, such as the famous eleventh edition of the Britannica.

Several companies specialize in research for public relations clients, including FIND/SVP, 500 Fifth Ave., N.Y. 10036; Information for Business, 730 Third Ave., N.Y. 10017; The Information Source, 1709 W. 8th St., Los Angeles, Calif. 90017 and Packaged Facts Information Service, 274 Madison Ave., N.Y. 10016.

The public relations library budget must include subscriptions to the many newsletters and magazines in public relations and related fields. These are described in the next chapter. If you hear or read about a publication in which you may be interested, send for a sample copy (generally free).

Gale Research Co., Book Tower, Detroit, Mich. 48226, publishes the Encyclopedia of Associations and many other books about speakers, acronyms, awards, statistics, faculty and other subjects relevant to public relations.

PUBLIC RELATIONS PERIODICALS

Public relations is a relatively small and new field, compared to advertising, publishing and other areas of communications. Many industries which are considerably larger than public relations have much fewer trade publications, and often one publication dominates the field and is required reading for almost every executive. Advertising Age, Editor & Publisher, Broadcasting, WWD (Women's Wear Daily), Automotive Age, Variety and Publisher's Weekly are the "bibles" of their fields. Such is not the case in public relations. Over a dozen periodicals are primarily or exclusively for public relations practitioners, ranging from weekly newsletters to quarterly journals. In addition, several dozen advertising, journalism, broadcasting and other media publications are relevant to public relations and include articles and news of interest and value to p.r. people.

Though no single periodical in the public relations field has the industry dominance or impact as WWD and other Fairchild publications have in their industries, several p.r. publications are extremely important. It is embarrassing to note that many public relations practitioners, including top executives, do not read any public relations periodicals. The exact opposite extreme is desirable. A major public relations agency or department should subscribe to many p.r. periodicals, and practitioners should read as many as possible in order to keep up-to-date with new techniques, media changes and other useful information. At the minimum, p.r. people should be familiar with the publications as publicity outlets and for use as an occasional reference.

Following is a catalog of over 30 publications which are oriented entirely to public relations or contain a sufficient amount of media information as to be considered as primary sources. The Saturday Review and other magazines often include articles which are relevant to the public relations field, but these are not included in this roundup.

A list of advertising publications appears in the first section of Bacon's Publicity Checker (14 East Jackson Blvd., Chicago 60604). Advertising and media publications *not* listed in Bacon's include Cleo (a TV publication, 30 E. 60 St., N.Y. 10022), Gavin Broadcast Report (1 Embarcadero Center, S.F. 94111) Hall Radio Report (30 Ten O'Clock Lane, Weston, Conn. 06880) and Media Report (4720 Montgomery Ave., Bethesda, Md. 20014).

Another media publication is Folio, a magnificently produced bimonthly "magazine for magazine management." Established in 1962, Folio also conducts an annual Book and Magazine Publishing Conference and Exposition. (J.J. Hanson, publisher and editor-in-chief, Box 697, New Canaan, Conn. 06840, $15.)

Toastmasters International is a well-known organization which provides its members with a friendly program to improve their communications abilities. Thus, the monthly magazine, The Toastmaster, features articles on speech making and other public relations subjects, but the folksy level generally lacks the details required by professional p.r. practitioners. However, the magazine is a bargain—only $3.60 a year for nonmembers. (Box 10400, Santa Ana, Calif. 92711.) Michael J. Snapp is editor.

General-interest consumer publications also are excluded. Time, Newsweek and The Saturday Review also have regular sections with media news. Also noteworthy are Phil Dougherty (The New York Times), George Lazarus (Chicago Tribune) and other advertising columnists who occasionally include public relations news.

Free "news guides" are published by The Patriot Ledger, Quincy, Mass. 02169; Asbury Park Press, Asbury Park, N.J. 07712, and The Washington Post, Wash., D.C. 20071.

Among the many financial relations publications, one newsletter which is useful (and free) is the Report to Corporate Management, published by the Investor and Corporate Communications Department of the New York Stock Exchange, 11 Wall Street, N.Y. 10005. A recent issue included an offer to provide house organ editors with an article about the role of the stock specialist, with photos of the individual specialist for the specific company.

Boardroom Reports (500 Fifth Ave., N.Y. 10036, $39) is avidly read by executives of large companies and owners of small businesses because of its collection of practical tips, including public relations and sales promotion. Publisher Martin Edelston deftly crams a great deal of material into the biweekly, 20-page newsletter.

Chapters and sections of PRSA, Publicity Clubs and other

organizations publish membership newsletters which are not covered in this chapter. The New York Times, Gannett Newspapers and other media publish house organs which include editorial format and personnel news of interest to publicists. Though it is possible to get on these mailing lists (alumni and advertisers are two categories which often are included), restricted-circulation publications are not described in this article. For example, Medical Communications is the excellent quarterly publication of the American Medical Writers Association.

One of the most specialized is the Speed Sport Public Relations Newsletter, an eight-page monthly mimeographed publication for motor sports promoters. Started in 1974, SSPRN is published ($15 a year) by Ernie and Marilyn Saxton of Ernie Saxton and Associates, Box 795, Langhorne, Pa. 19047.

Among the offbeat publications which may be useful but are not p.r.-oriented is Sidney Shore's unique four-page monthly newsletter called Creativity In Action ($50 a year, Box 272, Roslyn, N.Y. 11576).

The author personally subscribes to all except two of the following publications, as well as many other periodicals. Of course, some of the publications are scanned, and others are avidly read. Some of the publications are read at leisure, and others are read upon receipt and used as work aids.

If you are not familiar with these publications, this catalog may entice and enlighten you. Almost all publishers will send you a free sample copy, or you can find most of these periodicals at major libraries, particularly at universities with public relations departments. Many of these publications are available at the PRSA library in New York.

Once you subscribe to some or all of these publications, you'll not only find time to read them, but you may wonder how you ever functioned without them.

The prices of these periodicals range from zero to $96 a year. Since a few of them (e.g., Business Wire Newsletter) are sent only to members, and the subscription price is included in the dues, it's difficult to compute the total cost of all of these publications. Several publications cost less than the stated price if subscriptions are prepaid or entered for two or three years, and almost all will refund the balance of a subscription if you cancel. Of course, prices are subject to change (generally upward).

The total cost to subscribe to all of these publications is over $900 a year. If you think this is a lot of money, note the cost of an annual subscription to the National Journal, a weekly collection of article abstracts published in Washington, D.C. It's $300. Of course, you can save $30 with prepayment or try a six-month subscription for $150, less $15 for prepayment.

Can you afford to subscribe to all of the following periodicals? Perhaps not. But do you know what you're missing? Can you afford to be ignorant?

Advertising Age
740 N. Rush St., Chicago, Ill. 60611
Rance Crain, Editor-In-Chief
$40

It is almost impossible to function in the advertising business without reading Ad Age. Thus, any marketing-oriented public relations student or professional must read this weekly newspaper. (This author has had two subscriptions for many years— one at the office and one at home!) Published on Mondays since 1930, Ad Age occasionally publishes feature articles bylined by public relations practitioners, but its greater value is its news, editorials, surveys and special sections with detailed data about advertisers and advertising agencies.

AIM Report
Accuracy In Media, Inc.
777 14th St., N.W., Wash., D.C. 20005
Reed Irvine, Chairman
$15

Accuracy in Media is a nonprofit organization which monitors publications and programs for fairness and accuracy. The orientation is decidedly conservative, and, as might be expected, AIM's favorite and continuing targets are the Eastern liberal media, notably The New York Times, Washington Post, the broadcast networks and various Washington columnists. AIM has been vitriolic in its criticisms of Jack Anderson, Daniel Schorr and others. Most subscribers are supporters of AIM, but a few are media buffs, journalists and academicians.

Another strongly-biased (also politically conservative) media newsletter is Talknews, published monthly by C.H. Freedman, 213 E. Broadway, N.Y. 10002. Mr. Freedman is a talk radio program buff, and the chatty four-page publication provides news and comments about Bob Grant (WOR, N.Y.), Steve Powers (WMCA, N.Y.), Pegeen Fitzgerald (WOR, N.Y.) and other favorites, together with criticisms and barbs about feminists, anti-gun proponents and others with whom he disagrees. An annual subscription is only $3.60.

Atlanta's PR/News World
Southeastern Press Relations Newswire
161 Peachtree St., Atlanta, Ga. 30303
Larry Keller, Editor
Free

A four-page newsletter, published sporadically several times a year, with news and comments about media in the Southeast, primarily Atlanta. Though a promotional vehicle for current and potential subscribers of this publicity Teletype service, the newsletter contains nothing about the publisher's service and is crammed with media personnel changes and unusually candid opinions. It's so well-written that many communicators in the Southeast would be willing to pay for it, and, in several respects, it is superior to some of the national newsletters.

Business Wire Newsletter
235 Montgomery St., San Francisco, Calif. 94104
Lorry I. Lokey, General Manager and Editor
Free

Business Wire is a private Teletype service, with offices in San Francisco, Los Angeles, Seattle and Boston. BW's four-page monthly newsletter, which includes promotional material, is one of the most up-to-date, comprehensive regional media publications in the country. Its circulation (about 1500) is limited to Business Wire members and key editors on the circuit, and Lorry Lokey has resisted the temptation to provide it to others, including many Eastern publicists who are eager to become paying subscribers. In addition to dozens of items about media personnel changes (including bureau chiefs, syndicated columnists and others of national interest), the newsletter also features candid comments about problems of publishers, broadcasters and publicists.

Channels
Public Relations Society of America
845 Third Ave., N.Y. 10022
Don Bates, Editor
$24

Founded in 1923 by the National Public Relations Council of Health and Welfare Services, Channels is the oldest newsletter in the public relations field. NPRC was a public relations clearing house for health, welfare, educational and other nonprofit organizations. In 1976, it changed its name to the National Communication Council for Human Services, and in 1977 the Council consolidated its membership with the Public Relations Society of America.

Don Bates, who had been executive director of the Council, now edits Channels, a monthly mix of news and features on nonprofit agency public relations, management and fund raising.

Columbia Journalism Review
700 Journalism Bldg., Columbia University, N.Y. 10027
Spencer Klaw, Editor
$14

In 1961, the Columbia University Graduate School of Journalism started a bimonthly publication, to be a national monitor of print and broadcast media. The credo was stated in an editorial in the first issue.

"To assess the performance of journalism in all its forms, to call attention to its shortcomings and strengths, and to help

define—or redefine—standards of honest, responsible service
. . . to help stimulate continuing improvement in the profession
and to speak out for what is right, fair, and decent."

The magazine, which now has a circulation of over 35,000, has
fulfilled its mission in a lively manner. Though it is not as
muckraking as More, its articles have broad popular appeal, and
it is surprising that CJR is not as well-known as it should be
among public relations people. Could it be something as simple
as its omission from Bacon's Directory?

A recent issue included articles by Walter Cronkite, Daniel
Schorr, Judith Hennessee (contributing editor of More), Ronald
Kriss (senior editor at Time) and others. The magazine's first
editor, James Boylan, took a leave of absence in 1973, to earn a
Ph.D., returned in 1976, and then left in 1979.

A popular feature is a collection of "darts and laurels" (to
media) and other comment.

Contacts
Larimi Communications Associates
151 E. 50 St., N.Y. 10022
Michael M. Smith, Editor and Publisher
$105

Started in 1976, Contacts is a four-page weekly newsletter for
publicists about print and electronic media opportunities. It's
sort of a combination of Party Line and Media News Keys, with
odds and ends about media personnel changes and editorial
needs of editors and broadcasters. The information often
appears after similar data appeared in the competing publications, but Contacts sometimes has exclusives, and, more
important, almost every issue includes a detailed description of a
major publication or program. For example, a recent description of Popular Science featured a list of home addresses of
automotive, electronic and other specialists who are regular
contributors, and other valuable tips and data for publicists,
combined with a general introduction.

Larimi also publishes two directories, Television Contacts and
Radio Contacts.

The Corporate Communications Report
112 E. 31 St., N.Y. 10016
Richard Blodgett, Editor
$65

A 12-page bimonthly newsletter, published since 1969 by
Richard A. Lewis and Richard Blodgett, Corporate Communications Report is designed "to help the chief executive
officer and his key advisors communicate effectively with
stockholders and the financial community. Though called a
newsletter, it really is a mini-magazine in that each issue
generally consists of one or more articles on the same subject,

and there is none of the typical news item format of newsletters. The articles generally are not oriented to public relations in the same way that p.r. publications treat financial relations. For example, a recent issue discussed how companies are calculating and reporting replacement costs of plants, equipment, inventory and included a 13-point checklist with details about footnotes in reports to the SEC.

This carefully researched "newsletter" can be extremely useful to accountants, lawyers and financial relations specialists who work with large publicly owned companies.

Corporate Public Issues
105 Old Long Ridge Rd., Stamford, Conn. 06903
W. Howard Chase, Publisher and Editor
$96

Co-founder and past president of PRSA, W. Howard Chase indeed is a distinguished leader in the public relations field. His career combines journalism (editor of the Des Moines Register & Tribune from 1936 to 1938), public relations agencies (president of his own firm and others), companies (v.p. of American Can) and on and on.

In 1976, Dr. Chase (he also is a social scientist with academic credentials which include a Ph.D. degree!) started Corporate Public Issues, a semimonthly, four-to-six-page newsletter on the theory and practice of public policy management. Consumerism, environmental problems, inflation and other contemporary issues are discussed in a forthright manner. Primarily for government officials and industry management, the newsletter is unique' in the public relations realm it its focus on government and public affairs, labor relations, social responsibility and "issue management."

An incidental note about another unique aspect of CPI—it is the only p.r. newsletter which pays honoraria for invited case histories. More important is the publisher's philosophy, as stated recently in a personal letter: "I have grown increasingly disturbed at the status quo syndrome that characterizes the literature we buy. In this age of politicization and populism, traditional approaches are inadequate. Either public relations and its satellites—public affairs, communications, government relations, etc.—becomes a management science and a systems management process, or it is very likely to go the way of the buggy whip."

Editor & Publisher
575 Lexington Ave., N.Y. 10022
Robert V. Brown, Publisher and Editor
Jerome H. Walker Jr., Managing Editor
$35

The weekly bible of the daily newspaper field, Editor &

Publisher features data about new publications, syndicates, supplements and other print media, editorial personnel changes and a variety of news about the fourth estate. Some of the information turns up a few weeks later in Party Line and other public relations newsletters. Editor & Publisher contains so much about journalism, ranging from media demographics to production techniques, that it is a key resource for public relations practitioners.

The Editorial Eye
Editorial Experts, Inc.
5905 Pratt St., Alexandria, VA 22310
Laura Horowitz, Publisher
$45

An eight-page newsletter, this informal publication is crammed with tips, tests, listings and other material for editors and other communicators, including pragmatic advice for typists and word processors. 15 issues a year.

editors newsletter
Box 774, N.Y. 10010
Walter G. Anderson
$28

A four-page monthly compilation of news and comments about trends and techniques of business communications. Of greatest use to house organ editors, the publication is a junior version of the Ragan Report.

The Gallagher Report
230 Park Ave., N.Y. 10017
Bernard P. Gallagher, Editor-in-Chief
Cynthia A. Billings, Editor
$96

A confidential letter to marketing, sales, advertising and media executives, this four-page publication covers public relations only peripherally, but it is extremely valuable for its data and comments about media and advertisers. The publication is a combination of Winchellese gossip, pungent top-of-the-mountain predictions, colorful descriptions of marketing executives and other material which often is entertaining, controversial and informative. Product managers and other marketing executives sometimes bristle at Bernie Gallagher's advice, but Gallagher's record of accurate predictions is higher than ever attained by Walter Winchell. His special interest is media, particularly magazines, and the Gallagher Report often is the first to point out problem areas in seemingly successful consumer publications. Gallagher's pithy, personal style features nicknames (often alliterative and pejorative), staccato phrases and a dizzying, but effective, mixture of statistics and opinions. Occasional enclosures generally consist of salaries of executives or other data obtained by Gallagher mail surveys, including circulation and other media data.

Gallagher also publishes The President's Report, which has a similar content and flavor. The Gallagher staff, a big operation by newsletter standards, includes a managing and associate editor. They are keenly on the lookout for confidential tips and scoops and, as might be expected, dwell more on problems than successes. The publications are interested in news releases and often conduct interviews, but this is not a puff sheet or repository of personnel announcements or other routine publicity.

Hope Reports Perspective
919 S. Winston Rd., Rochester, N.Y. 14618
Tom Hope, Publisher and Editor
$30

A former market analyst at Eastman Kodak, Tom Hope has operated since 1970 a market research and publishing company which specializes in the audiovisual industry. If your company is a major producer, distributor or user of filmstrips, motion pictures, tapes and other AV materials, you should know about the Hope Reports.

The eight-page bimonthly newsletter, published since 1975, ranges from eight to 16 pages and features detailed analyses of video discs, cassettes and other equipment for exhibits, training and public relations. The publication does not report on personnel or other industry news and concentrates on statistical data and commentary about AV techniques and products.

Mr. and Mrs. Hope also publish quarterly and annual surveys and detailed reports on AV products and services.

Impact
203 N. Wabash Ave., Chicago, IL 60601
Robert Leon Baker, Editor
$18

Monthly four-page newsletter on trends, techniques and tools for communicators. Each issue is devoted to a single subject, such as "25 Tips for Taking Great Pictures."

Jack O'Dwyer's Newsletter
271 Madison Ave., N.Y. 10016
Jack O'Dwyer, Publisher and Editor
$70

Former New York Journal-American reporter Jack O'Dwyer competes with pr reporter and Public Relations News (both have larger circulations) by taking a totally different approach from these establishment publications. Jack is an independent who feels free to criticize public relations organizations and individuals. As a maverick, he's generally more entertaining and easy to read. His newsletter is more oriented to gossip and opinions and makes no attempt to provide case histories or service material. O'Dwyer diligently covers the New York beat, particularly p.r. agencies. Much like Bernard Gallagher, O'Dwyer is an investigative reporter who ignores routine news in favor of scoops. He also publishes two unique directories, one about public relations agencies and the other about public relations departments.

Journal of Communication
Annenberg School of Communication,
University of Pennsylvania
3620 Walnut St., Philadelphia, Pa. 19103
George Gerbner, editor
$15

Established in 1957, the Journal of Communication is a quarterly publication for psychologists, sociologists, political and social scientists, philosophers, academic journalists and others involved in theory, research, policy and practice of communication. Public relations practitioners can benefit considerably from such articles as Gossip as Social Communication, Humor as Communication, What is News, Radio as the People's Medium, Foreign News in the American Media, Conversations in Public Places, The Cable Fable and Nonverbal Communication. Many PR practitioners prefer to skim read and are impatient with footnotes and format of academic articles. The Journal of Communication is well worth the slight effort to read it, and it is surprisingly stimulating and easy to appreciate. A recent article by Marshall McLuhan started with this provocative sentence, "North Americans may well be the only people in the world who go outside to be alone and inside to be social."

Media Industry Newsletter
150 E. 52 St., N.Y. 10022
Leon Gary, Publisher
$58

News, features, research reports, predictions and candid opinions about publishers and broadcasters are crisply reported in this eight-page weekly newsletter. It is primarily of interest to advertising, marketing and media people, and not specifically oriented to public relations.

Media News Keys
Television Index, Inc.
150 Fifth Ave., N.Y. 10011
Jerry Leichter, Editor and Publisher
$70

Originally a newsletter (called Publicity Record, one of the oldest publications in the p.r. field), Media News Keys is a weekly four-page compilation of leads, contacts, changes and other data about all media of interest to publicists. In some respects, it is similar to Party Line. (Both publications are highly recommended.) Party Line is a succinct collection of items, including requests from free-lance writers, magazine editors and other publicity contacts. Media News Keys includes fuller descriptions of each program or publication and is extremely useful in keeping media directories (such as New York Publicity Outlets) up-to-date. The compact 5½ x 8½ page size has an easy-to-read, two column format, which generally starts with descriptions of new radio and television programs (network and local, throughout the country) and ends with listings of the editorial staffs of major consumer and trade publications. A greater amount of space is devoted to broadcast rather than print media. (Party Line has an opposite orientation, which is another reason for subscribing to both.)

Jerry Leichter is an authority on the broadcast media and publishes two services in this field. One of them, Radio-TV Contact Service, is of particular value to publicists. It consists of 3 x 5 index cards, each with a description, including whom to contact, of radio and television programs which originate in New York. The basic packet and monthly listings are $27.50 a year. Much of the information also appears in Media News Keys, but the cards are extremely handy to use, and Media News Keys subscribers can get the cards for the reduced price of $22.

Jerry Leichter operates with a small staff, but he and his staff are much more careful, accurate and comprehensive than several other media directory publishers. Media News Keys rarely is advertised, and it is not listed in Bacon's Publicity Checker. The publisher does not conduct any direct mail or other promotion campaigns. As a result, many publicists, particularly those not in New York, are unaware of it. Once you see a copy, you'll appreciate it as indispensable to the working publicist.

Media Personnel Directory
Alan Abrams, Editor
Gale Research Co., Book Tower, Detroit, MI 48226
$28.

A new type of media directory, introduced in 1979, Media Personnel Directory, lists 7,500 names of editors, publishers, columnists, art directors, book reviewers, correspondents and other personnel of about 700 U.S. and foreign magazines and periodicals.

A brilliant idea, particularly since media people do change jobs and sometimes are hard to track down. Listings are alphabetical, by last name, together with job title, address and phone of publication, and, here's a clever addition—previous media affiliation (if known).

The book is only for personnel of magazines and periodicals. Undoubtedly, the clever people at Gale will add other media categories.

The Perry Letter
Perry Corporate Communications
Box 91247, Atlanta, Ga. 30344
Matt Phelon, Senior V.P.
Free

This four-page monthly newsletter states that the annual subscription price is $50, but actually it's sent free to annual report producers and other prospective customers of this graphics firm. Many subscribers would be willing to pay, because each issue consists of descriptions of over a dozen annual reports and other publications, including reproductions of the covers or other pages.

PR Aids' Party Line
PR Aids Inc.
221 Park Ave. So., N.Y. 10003
Richard Toohey, Publisher
Betty Yarmon, Managing Editor
$90

This one 8½ x 11 sheet (both sides) of paper, published weekly, is worth more than its weight in gold (particulary at the current depressed price of gold) to publicists. The staff—publicist Betty Yarmon, her husband, Morton (also a public relations executive), and managing editor Grace W. Weinstein (who also is a magazine writer) compiles a succinct roundup of current placement opportunities in all media. In a recent issue, for example, 12 items included descriptions of several new syndicated columns and magazines, information about the needs of a free-lance magazine writer and changes in contacts for interview guests at several radio and TV programs. Each item includes names, addresses, phone numbers and time deadlines, so that the newsletter serves as an insider's tip sheet. PR Aids is the country's largest publicity mailing service, but Party Line is an independent operation, and promotional material is restricted to a footnote area. Comes with three holes punched on the side, and indeed it is useful to save it in a binder or other file. Subscribers should get in the habit of reading it on receipt (generally Mondays) and using the information with alacrity.

pr reporter
PR Publishing Company, Inc.
Box 600, Exeter, N.H. 03833
Otto Lerbinger and Patrick Jackson, Editorial Board
$80

Charles H. Prout (now a public relations executive in Wisconsin) started pr reporter as a biweekly four-page newsletter in 1958 and two years later sold it to Robert Barbour. A former railroad p.r. man, Bob Barbour had moved from New York to the small town of Meriden, New Hampshire, to publish

Who's Who in Public Relations. In spite of its off-track location, Barbour managed to keep p r reporter, which he converted to a weekly, a useful combination of up-to-date news and folksy commentary. The publication, particularly with its news of personnel, accounts and activities in the public relations field, was somewhat similar in appearance and subject matter to Public Relations News, though it never came close in circulation. In 1975, Bob Barbour died, and in 1976, his widow, Eleanor Barbour, sold the company to a group headed by Otto Lerbinger, professor of public relations at Boston University, and Patrick Jackson, who operates a public relations agency in Epping, New Hampshire.

Dr. Lerbinger is one of the world's most prominent educators in the public relations field, and the changes include a deemphasis on personnel and other news, and the introduction of more comments on broad aspects of public affairs and communications. Supplements include a one-sheet bimonthly summary of articles in social science and other journals. However, the newsletter is not overwhelmingly academic, intellectual, esoteric or pedantic and actually has become livelier and more useful to all types of public relations practitioners.

Public Relations Journal
Public Relations Society of America
845 Third Ave., N.Y. 10022
Leo Northart, Editor
$9.50 (Free to PRSA members; $7.50 of the annual dues is for a subscription.)

The only monthly magazine in the public relations field, the Public Relations Journal has the largest circulation (12,500) of any p.r. publication. Since it is distributed to all PRSA members, the magazine tries to offer something for everyone. In the past, the articles sometimes were bland, not as detailed as those in PRQ and Public Relations Review, rarely were controversial and often were "puff pieces" by unpaid contributors who were promoting or were associated with the subject. In spite of these understandable limitations, the Journal often published important articles, and, during the last year, a new design and sharper editing have produced a much livelier product.

Unlike the PRSA newsletter, the Journal includes advertising, and this revenue, plus the nonprofit orientation, makes the subscription fee a bargain to members and nonmembers of PRSA. One of the most useful features is the collection of columns by the editor and a cadre of outside experts, including Alvin M. Hattal (Washington), Philip Murphy (film), Chester Burger (book reviews), Eugene Marlow (new media) and Edie Fraser (consumerism).

In addition to the monthly magazines, subscribers receive the PRSA Membership Register, generally at the end of July.

Public Relations News
127 E. 80 St., N.Y. 10021
Denny Griswold, Editor
$147.75

Denny Griswold started this weekly four-page newsletter in 1944. For many years, it has had the largest circulation of any newsletter in the public relations field. Mrs. Griswold has become a spokesperson for public relations throughout the world (her slogan, used as the signature in the newsletter, is PRoud to Serve PR), and she is extremely active, energetic and passionate in her devotion to the field.

The first half of each issue is devoted to news and comments about public relations events, accounts and people. The two-column format, with considerable underlining, is easy to scan. The second section consists of a case study, with details about materials and results of recent campaigns, projects and special events.

Denny Griswold truly deserves the tributes she has received for her accomplishments, though some subscribers occasionally feel that the newsletter is conceited and self-serving, and has too much thumping for p.r. and not enough objectivity and candor. However, the case studies are well-researched and are not "publicity handouts," and the publisher has earned infinite praise for her conscientiousness, hard work, loyalty and contributions to the professionalism of public relations.

Public Relations Quarterly
44 W. Market St., Rhinebeck, N.Y. 12572
Howard Penn Hudson, Editor-Publisher
Mary Elizabeth Hudson, Associate Publisher
$12

Is a 32-page magazine worth $3 a copy? PRQ is expensive, in comparison with Public Relations Journal and most other public relations periodicals. However, PRQ often publishes in-depth articles with detailed advice and comments, and it is a useful component of the public relations library.

Mr. and Mrs. Hudson also operate the Newsletter Clearing House, a newsletter-consulting business, and publish the Newsletter on Newsletters ($36 a year, monthly) and a newsletter directory. As if that weren't enough, they also have several public relations clients and publish Hudson's Washington Directory. At $35 a copy (including three lists of revisions sent during the year), the annual Hudson's Washington Directory is a superb bargain. It lists over 2500 members of the Washington press corps and is one of the indispensable media directories for publicists.

Public Relations Review
College of Journalsim, University of Maryland, College Park, Md. 20742
$10

In 1975, the Foundation for Public Relations Research and Education started this quarterly journal to build a bridge between public relations and social and behavioral science. Articles, which generally are by social scientists, often report or comment on research. The format and writing style is not as heavy as in some academic journals. Public Relations Review definitely is *the* journal of research in the public relations and communications field, and the articles reflect high standards of scholarship combined with practical applications.

The publication is printed on high-quality paper in an attractive, easy-to-read text format. The Foundation is an independent, nonprofit organization, established in 1956 by members of the Public Relations Society of America.

Publicist
PR Aids Inc.
221 Park Ave., N.Y. 10003
Lee Levitt, Editor
Free

Inaugurated in 1976, Publicist is a snappy-looking tabloid newspaper sent free to just about every working publicist in the country. The sponsors are eight major companies (including the PR Aids mailing service) who sell to publicists, and the trade journal is filled with house ads. Between the ads is an amazingly good collection of well-written, easy-to-read, how-to-do-it studies, case histories, personality profiles and other articles. Surprisingly, the material often is not found in any other publication, and Publicist thus has quickly established itself as a major resource in the field. In fact, it's so good that many readers would be willing to pay for it, which is one of the highest compliments one can give to a controlled-circulation publication.

Publishers' Weekly
1180 Ave. of the Americas, N.Y. 10036
Arnold W. Erlich, Editor-in-Chief
$33

Established in 1852, Publishers' Weekly is the bible of the book publishing industry. Since books often are publicized, PW includes a section on media, with information of value to all publicists.

The publisher, R.R. Bowker (a Xerox Education Company), also publishes the annual Literary Market Place, one of the most useful reference books in the public relations field. Priced at $19.95, it is a bargain.

Other Bowker reference books include Ulrich's International Periodicals Directory ($46.50).

The Quill
35 E. Wacker Drive, Chicago, Ill. 60601
Charles Long, Editor
$10

Published since 1912 by Sigma Delta Chi (The Society of Professional Journalists), the Quill is a popular (circulation 30,000) monthly magazine with news about members and chapters, as well as articles about print media. The orientation is to journalism students and professionals, ranging from high school newspapers to wire services, and the material generally is of interest to public relations practitioners, but not as timely or directly relevant as Editor & Publisher.

The Ragan Report
Lawrence Ragan Communications, Inc.
407 S. Dearborn St., Chicago, Ill. 60605
Lawrence Ragan, Editor
$50

A four-page weekly newsletter, with each issue supplemented by a two- to four-page commentary by an outside contributor. The newsletter is a potpourri of news and views, mostly about employee magazines and other special-interest publications. The greatest value is to editors, and the emphasis is on improving the quality of writing. Larry Ragan is a publishing consultant and lecturer, and is an excellent teacher, who conducts workshops for editors which feature detailed, pragmatic critiques. The newsletter includes many of these no-punches-pulled critiques, plus news about new p.r.-oriented publications and projects. The enclosures are by a cadre of regular contributors, who share the same no-nonsense orientation, including visual consultant Phil Douglis, writer Milton Moskowitz and typography experts Edmund C. Arnold and Alden S. Wood.

Social Science Monitor
Communication Research Associates, Inc.
7338 Baltimore Blvd., College Park, Md. 20740
$64 ($172 for three years)

Started in 1979, Social Science Monitor is a monthly eight-page newsletter which translates the social and behavioral sciences for use by public relations, advertising and marketing people.

Professor Otto Lerbinger does this in a two-page supplement (Purview) enclosed with Public Relations Reporter. Howard Chase has a social science orientation in his newsletter, and others have done this in the past. Avram E. King was unsuccessful in publishing Predictive Communications, which folded along with his Practical Public Relations. Communications Management Systems, headed by clipping analyst Paul Lewis, no longer publishes Management & Society, which was a monthly survey of research for public relations.

Thus, Social Science Monitor now is the only publication totally devoted to linking social and behavioral science research with the public relations practitioner. The editor, Ray E. Hiebert, is extremely well-qualified for this difficult task.

Dr. Hiebert is dean of the College of Journalism at the University of Maryland and author and editor of more than a dozen books on communication and public relations. He was a founder of Public Relations Review, the quarterly journal published at the University of Maryland by the Foundation for Public Relations Research and Education. The foundation was started in 1956 by Dr. Hiebert and other PRSA members, and he was selected PRSA Educator of the Year in 1978.

In this sense, the newsletter emanates from the Public Relations Review, but the newsletter has a very pragmatic orientation, and its sources include Playboy, Boston Globe and other mass media, as well as Social Science Research and other academic journals.

Washington Journalism Review
2233 Wisconsin Ave., N.W., Washington, D.C. 20007
Jessica Cato, Pres., Ray White, Editor
$16

Started in 1977 as a project of the Washington Media Education Center, WJR has become a lively review of journalism, with much of the punch of the defunct More. The orientation is to Washington-based media, which includes national publications and bureaus. The magazine is lavishly illustrated with color drawings. The beautiful layouts and sprightly writing make WJR quite lively, akin to New York, The Washingtonian and other city magazines.

When WJR started, Edwin Diamond (former media editor of Newsweek) was senior editor and an advisory board included Martin Agronsky, Ernest B. Fergurson, Frank Mankiewicz, Clark Mollenhoff, Sander Vanocur, Nicholas von Hoffman and other celebrities.

In the lead article in the premiere issue, Larry McMurty wrote, "One would also hope to see, in this magazine, something more than tittle and tattle about journalists and journalistic practice."

WJR has changed considerably since its first issues. No longer a nonprofit operation, WJR has undergone considerable personnel and other changes. The highly favorable result has been something considerably more than tittle and tattle.

Writer's Digest
9933 Alliance Road, Cincinnati, Ohio 45242
John Brady, Editor
$7.95

Established in 1919, Writer's Digest is primarily for beginning and professional free-lance writings, from fillers and poetry to magazine articles and books. Most of the articles are not likely to be of value to publicists. However, the descriptions of new and offbeat media often include material not found elsewhere. Some of this turns up, in abbreviated form, in Party Line and other publicity publications, but at $7.95 for 12 monthly issues, Writer's Digest is a bargain. (The editor is not related to Richard Weiner.)

The Writer (8 Arlington Street, Boston 02116, A.S. Burack, Editor, $9) is a similar monthly magazine. Established in 1887, The Writer has about half the circulation of Writer's Digest.

The Writer Report
4219 Las Cruces Way, Sacramento, CA 95825
Chuck Woodbury, Editor
$15

A monthly four-page newsletter for freelance nonfiction writers and photographers. Though publicists generally provide materials free instead of for a fee, this can be used, with other writers' publications to identify media.

CONCLUSION

We live in an era of communications, in which consumers and other recipients of information are bombarded with a variety of messages from a multitude of media. The most effective form of communication is still a two-way personal conversation between two people. However, advertisers and public relations professionals have to resort to such impersonal means of communication as direct mail, the purchase of time and space and, in order to obtain a third-party endorsement, rely on the news media and the other media where it is possible to obtain publicity.

The number of newspapers, magazines and other mass media publications is diminishing at the same time that the number of publicists and their output is increasing. It thus is more difficult than ever before for the average news release to be published.

The professional public relations practitioner can improve his efficiency in several ways, starting with the quality of his news releases. A major factor concerns the sending of a news release to all publications which might have an interest in the specific subject. Some publicists resolve this problem by mailing to a large number of publications, including many which are not likely to have an interest in the subject. This is wasteful, of course.

The opposite extreme—omission of mass mailings and reliance on individual contacts—also is likely to be inefficient. Some novices believe that media *contacts* are very important in the public relations field, and that publicists spend a lot of time taking out editors and broadcasters, and wining and dining them and winning their favor. Among threatrical press agents, contacts are alleged to be of considerable importance, and it is said that Walter Winchell and other famous columnists dealt only with "favored" press agents. Be that as it may, most

171

publicists can't rely only on media people whom they know on a personal basis. There simply are too many media, and the people at these media are constantly changing. And so, the contact is of lesser importance as compared to the content, timing and the knowledge of the techniques of the public relations field.

There are dozens of courses and books which deal with the theory and practice of public relations. Most rely on case histories and examples to describe the mechanical details of the practice of publicity.

This manual is a compilation of several hundred tips and other practical advice. Many aspects of the field are omitted, as they are covered in other books, and instead an attempt has been made to list succinctly how-to points and recommendations for use by the novice, as well as the experienced publicist.

Many of the opinions are subject to exceptions, particularly in the attempt to generalize and be more pragmatic and candid than is generally done in textbooks.

One subject which is rarely discussed is bribes. That is, payoffs by publicists to media people. Dishonesty exists among all people, but there is much less of it between publicists and media people than in most other fields. The subject of press junkets (often costing many hundreds of dollars per person), lunches (sometimes costing over $25 per person) and gifts (such as product samples) is complex, as the ethical difference between these exchanges and cash gratuities sometimes is fuzzy.

One of the wierdest instances of alleged press payola was revealed in 1977 in New West. The magazine article discribed a Los Angeles public relations man who conned quite a few businessmen into paying him in order to "purchase" articles in major magazines. Part of the cash was supposed to go to editors and reporters. The public relations man committed suicide, so it never was revealed if any journalists received the monies.

Though the successful professionals in the publicity field vary considerably in age, temperament, background, type of work, one almost universal factor is enthusiasm. The vagaries and frustrations of publicity often produce a weariness, but the capable publicist generally retains an affection and respect for the media and an enthusiastic interest in publicity. And this enthusiasm can be contagious.

REFERENCE AND RESOURCE DIRECTORY

The following list of media guide books and other commonly used services is extremely limited and refers only to those resources referred to in this book.

Ayer Directory of Publications
Ayerpress, 1 Bala Ave., Bala Cynwyd, Pa. 19004

Bacon's Publicity Checker
R.H. Bacon & Co., 14 E. Jackson Blvd., Chicago 60604

Broadcasting Yearbook
Broadcasting Publications, 1735 De Sales St., N.W.
Washington, D.C. 20036

Editor & Publisher International Year Book
Editor & Publisher, 575 Lexington Ave., N.Y. 10022

Hudson's Washington News Media Contacts Directory
2814 Pennsylvania Ave., N.W., Washington D.C. 20007

Literary Market Place
R.R. Bowker Co., 1180 Ave. of the Americas, N.Y. 10036

Media News Keys
150 Fifth Ave., 10011

New York Publicity Outlets (also TV Publicity Outlets)
Washington Depot, Conn. 06794

PR Aids
221 Park Avenue South, N.Y. 10003

PR Newswire, 150 E. 58 St., N.Y. 10022

Party Line
PR Aids, 221 Park Avenue South, N.Y. 10003

Professional's Guide to Public Relations Services
Richard Weiner, Inc., 888 Seventh Ave., N.Y. 10019

Radio-Television Contact Cards
Media News Keys, 150 Fifth Ave., N.Y. 10011

# # #

INDEX